The Collected Verse of A. B. Paterson

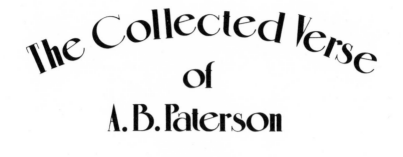

The Collected Verse
of
A. B. Paterson

With the original illustrations of
Norman Lindsay, Hal Gye & Lionel Lindsay

ANGUS & ROBERTSON PUBLISHERS

ANGUS & ROBERTSON PUBLISHERS
London • Sydney • Melbourne

First published by Angus & Robertson Publishers, Australia, 1921
This illustrated edition 1982
Reprinted 1983 (twice), 1984

Published by arrangement with the copyright owner

National Library of Australia
Cataloguing-in-publication data.

Paterson, A. B. (Andrew Barton), 1864–1941.
    The collected verse of A. B. Paterson.

    First published: Sydney: Angus & Robertson, 1921.
    ISBN 0 207 14676 4

    I. Title.

A821'.2

Printed in Hong Kong by Everbest Printing Co., Ltd.

ACKNOWLEDGEMENTS

Angus & Robertson Publishers acknowledge with thanks the Mitchell Library for access to photograph the original artwork of the Norman Lindsay covers and frontispiece illustration and the Hal Gye cover and title page vignette; and the owners for access to photograph the original artwork of Hal Gye's frontispiece illustration, Norman Lindsay's title page vignette and Lionel Lindsay's frontispiece illustration.

PUBLISHER'S NOTE

A. B. Paterson's three books of verse, *The Man from Snowy River* (1895), *Rio Grande* (1902) and *Saltbush Bill, J.P.* (1917) were reprinted many times before being combined in 1921 as *The Collected Verse of A. B. Paterson*. However, only one edition of each volume was published with the full splendour of colour jacket, frontispiece and title page illustrations. These were those published in 1917 by Angus & Robertson as "pocket editions for the trenches". Designed to fit the tunic pockets of the Anzacs, they were small (14.5 x 11.5 cm) books. Into their presentation was poured much love and care and, despite the necessary wartime frugality which generally restricted the use of all but monotone printing, the work of three outstanding illustrators was commissioned to be reproduced in full colour.

Most of those illustrated editions left the country never to return and so copies are today rare and access to these charming illustrations has been limited. Rarer still is the cover illustration (see opposite p. 96) prepared for *The Man from Snowy River* by Norman Lindsay but never before used. It illustrates "Angel Harrison's black gelding Pardon" from the ballad "Old Pardon the Son of Reprieve" which was the first of Paterson's work to attract significant attention when originally published in *The Bulletin*. However, George Robertson, publisher of A & R at that time, rejected this cover and suggested another (see opposite p. xvi) which Lindsay willingly agreed to. In a letter from Springwood in 1916 he wrote:

> Dear Robertson, I will do you another cover for *The Man from Snowy River*, for the truth is I was not at all satisfied with the one I sent, not from theological but technical reasons. I thought it was poorly executed, and though I had two shots at it the thing wouldn't come successfully. But I sent it, as I supposed you were in a hurry.
>
> But I was pleased with "Clancy"*. It seemed to me that I was fortunate in suggesting the dusty heat of this subject. I've been through Paterson again, and conclude that your suggestion for the cover is best. One can't get away from the horse in Banjo, so it's no use trying.

It is interesting to speculate on the effect these illustrations may have had on the troops — Norman Lindsay's dusty droving and

* See opposite p. 17

vii

homestead scenes, Lionel Lindsay's magnificent wild brumbies and his grandfatherly Saltbush surrounded by "little rouseabouts", Hal Gye's soldiers from an earlier conflict, ramrod straight on sentry duty or in the saddle. It is hoped that this edition of Paterson's poems, accompanied once again by the paintings of his illustrious contemporaries, will bring today's reader an experience of unalloyed delight.

A. B. Paterson
This handsome and popular young solicitor and sportsman was revealed,
with the first publication in book form of his poems,
to be "The Banjo" of *Bulletin* fame.
The immediate success of his volumes of verse was described
as "without parallel in Colonial literary annals" as he could claim
"a wider public than any English or American poet
of the time except Kipling".

Norman Lindsay

A prolific master of many trades, Norman Lindsay was equally
well respected for his oils, watercolours, etchings,
book illustration, cartoons, essays and novels.
He was also to gain the lasting affection of the children of many nations
for his bad-tempered, irrepressible *Puddin'*.

Hal Gye

Hal Gye had earned a reputation as a skilful cartoonist
when commissioned in 1916 to illustrate the work for which he is best known,
The Sentimental Bloke by C. J. Dennis. He followed the success of his larrikin
cherubs with the fanciful and grotesque illustrations
for *The Glugs of Gosh*, but soon thereafter returned to cartooning.
However he was later to emerge, under the nom de plume
of James Hackston, as a fine short-story writer.

Lionel Lindsay

The third son of the talented Lindsay family,
Lionel Arthur Lindsay was later to acquire a knighthood
for his services to art and an international reputation
as an etcher, wood-engraver, watercolourist,
journalist and art critic.

CONTENTS

I
THE MAN FROM SNOWY RIVER
AND OTHER VERSES

PRELUDE

I have gathered these stories afar
  In the wind and the rain,
In the land where the cattle-camps are,
  On the edge of the plain.
On the overland routes of the west,
  When the watches were long,
I have fashioned in earnest and jest
  These fragments of song.

They are just the rude stories one hears
  In sadness and mirth,
The records of wandering years—
  And scant is their worth.
Though their merits indeed are but slight,
  I shall not repine
If they give you one moment's delight,
  Old comrades of mine.

Norman Lindsay's jacket for
The Man from Snowy River

THE MAN
FROM SNOWY RIVER

THERE was movement at the station, for the word had passed
    around
  That the colt from old Regret had got away,
And had joined the wild bush horses—he was worth a thousand
    pound,
  So all the cracks had gathered to the fray.
All the tried and noted riders from the stations near and far
  Had mustered at the homestead overnight,
For the bushmen love hard riding where the wild bush horses are,
  And the stock-horse snuffs the battle with delight.

There was Harrison, who made his pile when Pardon won the cup,
  The old man with his hair as white as snow;
But few could ride beside him when his blood was fairly up—
  He would go wherever horse and man could go.
And Clancy of the Overflow came down to lend a hand,
  No better horseman ever held the reins;
For never horse could throw him while the saddle-girths would
    stand—
  He learnt to ride while droving on the plains.

And one was there, a stripling on a small and weedy beast;
  He was something like a racehorse undersized,
With a touch of Timor pony—three parts thoroughbred at least—
  And such as are by mountain horsemen prized.
He was hard and tough and wiry—just the sort that won't say die—
  There was courage in his quick impatient tread;
And he bore the badge of gameness in his bright and fiery eye,
  And the proud and lofty carriage of his head.

But still so slight and weedy, one would doubt his power to stay,
  And the old man said, "That horse will never do
For a long and tiring gallop—lad, you'd better stop away,
  Those hills are far too rough for such as you."
So he waited, sad and wistful—only Clancy stood his friend—
  "I think we ought to let him come," he said;
"I warrant he'll be with us when he's wanted at the end,
  For both his horse and he are mountain bred.

"He hails from Snowy River, up by Kosciusko's side,
   Where the hills are twice as steep and twice as rough;
Where a horse's hoofs strike firelight from the flint stones every
      stride,
   The man that holds his own is good enough.
And the Snowy River riders on the mountains make their home,
   Where the river runs those giant hills between;
I have seen full many horsemen since I first commenced to roam,
   But nowhere yet such horsemen have I seen."

So he went; they found the horses by the big mimosa clump,
   They raced away towards the mountain's brow,
And the old man gave his orders, "Boys, go at them from the jump,
   No use to try for fancy riding now.
And, Clancy, you must wheel them, try and wheel them to the right.
   Ride boldly, lad, and never fear the spills,
For never yet was rider that could keep the mob in sight,
   If once they gain the shelter of those hills."

So Clancy rode to wheel them—he was racing on the wing
   Where the best and boldest riders take their place,
And he raced his stock-horse past them, and he made the ranges ring
   With the stockwhip, as he met them face to face.
Then they halted for a moment, while he swung the dreaded lash,
   But they saw their well-loved mountain full in view,
And they charged beneath the stockwhip with a sharp and sudden
      dash,
   And off into the mountain scrub they flew.

Then fast the horsemen followed, where the gorges deep and black
   Resounded to the thunder of their tread,
And the stockwhips woke the echoes, and they fiercely answered
      back
   From cliffs and crags that beetled overhead.
And upward, ever upward, the wild horses held their way,
   Where mountain ash and kurrajong grew wide;
And the old man muttered fiercely, "We may bid the mob good day,
   No man can hold them down the other side."

When they reached the mountain's summit, even Clancy took a
      pull—
   It well might make the boldest hold their breath;
The wild hop scrub grew thickly, and the hidden ground was full
   Of wombat holes, and any slip was death.

But the man from Snowy River let the pony have his head,
  And he swung his stockwhip round and gave a cheer,
And he raced him down the mountain like a torrent down its bed,
  While the others stood and watched in very fear.

He sent the flint-stones flying, but the pony kept his feet,
  He cleared the fallen timber in his stride,
And the man from Snowy River never shifted in his seat—
  It was grand to see that mountain horseman ride.
Through the stringy barks and saplings, on the rough and broken
      ground,
  Down the hillside at a racing pace he went;
And he never drew the bridle till he landed safe and sound
  At the bottom of that terrible descent.

He was right among the horses as they climbed the farther hill,
  And the watchers on the mountain, standing mute,
Saw him ply the stockwhip fiercely; he was right among them still,
  As he raced across the clearing in pursuit.
Then they lost him for a moment, where two mountain gullies met
  In the ranges—but a final glimpse reveals
On a dim and distant hillside the wild horses racing yet,
  With the man from Snowy River at their heels.

And he ran them single-handed till their sides were white with foam;
  He followed like a bloodhound on their track,
Till they halted, cowed and beaten; then he turned their heads for
      home,
  And alone and unassisted brought them back.
But his hardy mountain pony he could scarcely raise a trot,
  He was blood from hip to shoulder from the spur;
But his pluck was still undaunted, and his courage fiery hot,
  For never yet was mountain horse a cur.

And down by Kosciusko, where the pine-clad ridges raise
  Their torn and rugged battlements on high,
Where the air is clear as crystal, and the white stars fairly blaze
  At midnight in the cold and frosty sky,
And where around the Overflow the reed-beds sweep and sway
  To the breezes, and the rolling plains are wide,
The Man from Snowy River is a household word today,
  And the stockmen tell the story of his ride.

OLD PARDON,
THE SON OF REPRIEVE

You never heard tell of the story?
    Well, now, I can hardly believe!
Never heard of the honour and glory
    Of Pardon, the son of Reprieve?
But maybe you're only a Johnnie
    And don't know a horse from a hoe?
Well, well, don't get angry, my sonny,
    But, really, a young un should know.

They bred him out back on the "Never",
    His mother was Mameluke breed.
To the front—and then stay there—was ever
    The root of the Mameluke creed.
He seemed to inherit their wiry
    Strong frames—and their pluck to receive—
As hard as a flint and as fiery
    Was Pardon, the son of Reprieve.

We ran him at many a meeting
    At crossing and gully and town,
And nothing could give him a beating—
    At least when our money was down.
For weight wouldn't stop him, nor distance,
    Nor odds, though the others were fast;
He'd race with a dogged persistence,
    And wear them all down at the last.

At the Turon the Yattendon filly
    Led by lengths at the mile-and-a-half,
And we all began to look silly,
    While her crowd were starting to laugh;
But the old horse came faster and faster,
    His pluck told its tale, and his strength,
He gained on her, caught her, and passed her,
    And won it, hands-down, by a length.

And then we swooped down on Menindie
    To run for the President's Cup;
Oh! that's a sweet township—a shindy
    To them is board, lodging, and sup.

Eye-openers they are, and their system
  Is never to suffer defeat;
It's "win, tie, or wrangle"—to best 'em
  You must lose 'em, or else it's "dead heat".

We strolled down the township and found 'em
  At drinking and gaming and play;
If sorrows they had, why they drowned 'em,
  And betting was soon under way.
Their horses were good uns and fit uns,
  There was plenty of cash in the town;
They backed their own horses like Britons,
  And, Lord! how *we* rattled it down!

With gladness we thought of the morrow,
  We counted our wages with glee,
A simile homely to borrow—
  "There was plenty of milk in our tea."
You see we were green; and we never
  Had even a thought of foul play,
Though we well might have known that the clever
  Division would "put us away".

Experience *docet*, they tell us,
  At least so I've frequently heard;
But, "dosing" or "stuffing", those fellows
  Were up to each move on the board:
They got to his stall—it is sinful
  To think what such villains will do—
And they gave him a regular skinful
  Of barley—green barley—to chew.

He munched it all night, and we found him
  Next morning as full as a hog—
The girths wouldn't nearly meet round him;
  He looked like an overfed frog.
We saw we were done like a dinner—
  The odds were a thousand to one
Against Pardon turning up winner,
  'Twas cruel to ask him to run.

We got to the course with our troubles,
    A crestfallen couple were we;
And we heard the "books" calling the doubles—
    A roar like the surf of the sea;
And over the tumult and louder
    Rang "Any price Pardon, I lay!"
Says Jimmy, "The children of Judah
    Are out on the warpath today."

Three miles in three heats:—Ah, my sonny,
    The horses in those days were stout,
They had to run well to win money;
    I don't see such horses about.
Your six-furlong vermin that scamper
    Half-a-mile with their feather-weight up,
They wouldn't earn much of their damper
    In a race like the President's Cup.

The first heat was soon set a-going;
    The Dancer went off to the front;
The Don on his quarters was showing,
    With Pardon right out of the hunt.
He rolled and he weltered and wallowed—
    You'd kick your hat faster, I'll bet;
They finished all bunched, and he followed
    All lathered and dripping with sweat.

But troubles came thicker upon us,
    For while we were rubbing him dry
The stewards came over to warn us:
    "We hear you are running a bye!
If Pardon don't spiel like tarnation
    And win the next heat—if he can—
He'll earn a disqualification;
    Just think over *that* now, my man!"

Our money all gone and our credit,
    Our horse couldn't gallop a yard;
And then people thought that *we* did it
    It really was terribly hard.
We were objects of mirth and derision
    To folks in the lawn and the stand,
And the yells of the clever division
    Of "Any price Pardon!" were grand.

We still had a chance for the money,
　　Two heats still remained to be run:
If both fell to us—why, my sonny,
　　The clever division were done.
And Pardon was better, we reckoned,
　　His sickness was passing away,
So we went to the post for the second
　　And principal heat of the day.

They're off and away with a rattle,
　　Like dogs from the leashes let slip,
And right at the back of the battle
　　He followed them under the whip.
They gained ten good lengths on him quickly
　　He dropped right away from the pack;
I tell you it made me feel sickly
　　To see the blue jacket fall back.

Our very last hope had departed—
　　We thought the old fellow was done,
When all of a sudden he started
　　To go like a shot from a gun.
His chances seemed slight to embolden
　　Our hearts; but, with teeth firmly set,
We thought, "Now or never! The old un
　　May reckon with some of 'em yet."

Then loud rose the war-cry for Pardon;
　　He swept like the wind down the dip,
And over the rise by the garden
　　The jockey was done with the whip.
The field was at sixes and sevens—
　　The pace at the first had been fast—
And hope seemed to drop from the heavens,
　　For Pardon was coming at last.

And how he did come! It was splendid;
　　He gained on them yards every bound,
Stretching out like a greyhound extended,
　　His girth laid right down on the ground.
A shimmer of silk in the cedars
　　As into the running they wheeled,
And out flashed the whips on the leaders,
　　For Pardon had collared the field.

Then right through the ruck he was sailing—
    I knew that the battle was won—
The son of Haphazard was failing,
    The Yattendon filly was done;
He cut down The Don and The Dancer,
    He raced clean away from the mare—
He's in front! Catch him now if you can, sir!
    And up went my hat in the air!

Then loud from the lawn and the garden
    Rose offers of "Ten to one *on!*"
"Who'll bet on the field? I back Pardon!"
    No use; all the money was gone.
He came for the third heat light-hearted,
    A-jumping and dancing about;
The others were done ere they started
    Crestfallen, and tired, and worn out.

He won it, and ran it much faster
    Than even the first, I believe;
Oh, he was the daddy, the master,
    Was Pardon, the son of Reprieve.
He showed 'em the method of travel—
    The boy sat still as a stone—
They never could see him for gravel;
    He came in hard-held, and alone.

      .   .   .   .   .

But he's old—and his eyes are grown hollow
    Like me, with my thatch of the snow;
When he dies, then I hope I may follow,
    And go where the racehorses go.
I don't want no harping nor singing—
    Such things with my style don't agree;
Where the hoofs of the horses are ringing
    There's music sufficient for me.

And surely the thoroughbred horses
    Will rise up again and begin
Fresh races on far-away courses,
    And p'raps they might let me slip in.
It would look rather well the race-card on
    'Mongst Cherubs and Seraphs and things,
"Angel Harrison's black gelding Pardon,
    Blue halo, white body and wings."

And if they have racing hereafter,
  (And who is to say they will not?)
When the cheers and the shouting and laughter
  Proclaim that the battle grows hot;
As they come down the racecourse a-steering,
  He'll rush to the front, I believe;
And you'll hear the great multitude cheering
  For Pardon, the son of Reprieve.

CLANCY
OF THE OVERFLOW

I HAD written him a letter which I had, for want of better
  Knowledge, sent to where I met him down the Lachlan years ago;
He was shearing when I knew him, so I sent the letter to him,
  Just on spec, addressed as follows, "Clancy, of The Overflow".

And an answer came directed in a writing unexpected
  (And I think the same was written with a thumb-nail dipped
    in tar);
'Twas his shearing mate who wrote it, and *verbatim* I will quote it:
  "Clancy's gone to Queensland droving, and we don't know where
    he are."

        .   .   .   .   .

In my wild erratic fancy visions come to me of Clancy
  Gone a-droving "down the Cooper" where the Western drovers go;
As the stock are slowly stringing, Clancy rides behind them singing,
  For the drover's life has pleasures that the townsfolk never know.

And the bush has friends to meet him, and their kindly voices
    greet him
  In the murmur of the breezes and the river on its bars,
And he sees the vision splendid of the sunlit plains extended,
  And at night the wondrous glory of the everlasting stars.

        .   .   .   .   .

I am sitting in my dingy little office, where a stingy
  Ray of sunlight struggles feebly down between the houses tall,
And the foetid air and gritty of the dusty, dirty city,
  Through the open window floating, spreads its foulness over all.

And in place of lowing cattle, I can hear the fiendish rattle
  Of the tramways and the buses making hurry down the street;
And the language uninviting of the gutter children fighting
  Comes fitfully and faintly through the ceaseless tramp of feet.

And the hurrying people daunt me, and their pallid faces haunt me
  As they shoulder one another in their rush and nervous haste,
With their eager eyes and greedy, and their stunted forms and
    weedy,
  For townsfolk have no time to grow, they have no time to waste.

And I somehow rather fancy that I'd like to change with Clancy,
  Like to take a turn at droving where the seasons come and go,
While he faced the round eternal of the cash-book and the journal—
  But I doubt he'd suit the office, Clancy, of The Overflow.

CONROY'S GAP

THIS was the way of it, don't you know—
   Ryan was "wanted" for stealing sheep,
And never a trooper, high or low,
   Could find him—catch a weasel asleep!
Till Trooper Scott, from the Stockman's Ford—
   A bushman, too, as I've heard them tell—
Chanced to find him drunk as a lord
   Round at the Shadow of Death Hotel.

D'you know the place? It's a wayside inn,
   A low grog-shanty—a bushman trap,
Hiding away in its shame and sin
   Under the shelter of Conroy's Gap—
Under the shade of that frowning range
   The roughest crowd that ever drew breath—
Thieves and rowdies, uncouth and strange,
   Were mustered round at the "Shadow of Death".

The trooper knew that his man would slide
   Like a dingo pup, if he saw the chance;
And with half a start on the mountain side
   Ryan would lead him a merry dance.
Drunk as he was when the trooper came,
   To him that did not matter a rap—
Drunk or sober, he was the same,
   The boldest rider in Conroy's Gap.

"I want you, Ryan," the trooper said,
   "And listen to me, if you dare resist,
So help me heaven, I'll shoot you dead!"
   He snapped the steel on his prisoner's wrist,
And Ryan, hearing the handcuffs click,
   Recovered his wits as they turned to go,
For fright will sober a man as quick
   As all the drugs that the doctors know.

There was a girl in that shanty bar
   Went by the name of Kate Carew,
Quiet and shy as the bush girls are,
   But ready-witted and plucky, too.

She loved this Ryan, or so they say,
  And passing by, while her eyes were dim
With tears, she said in a careless way,
  "The Swagman's round in the stable, Jim."

Spoken too low for the trooper's ear,
  Why should she care if he heard or not?
Plenty of swagmen far and near—
  And yet to Ryan it meant a lot.
That was the name of the grandest horse
  In all the district from east to west;
In every show ring, on every course,
  They always counted The Swagman best.

He was a wonder, a raking bay—
  One of the grand old Snowdon strain—
One of the sort that could race and stay
  With his mighty limbs and his length of rein.
Born and bred on the mountain side,
  He could race through scrub like a kangaroo;
The girl herself on his back might ride,
  And The Swagman would carry her safely through.

He would travel gaily from daylight's flush
  Till after the stars hung out their lamps;
There was never his like in the open bush,
  And never his match on the cattle-camps.
For faster horses might well be found
  On racing tracks, or a plain's extent,
But few, if any, on broken ground
  Could see the way that The Swagman went.

When this girl's father, old Jim Carew,
  Was droving out on the Castlereagh
With Conroy's cattle, a wire came through
  To say that his wife couldn't live the day.
And he was a hundred miles from home,
  As flies the crow, with never a track
Through plains as pathless as ocean's foam;
  He mounted straight on The Swagman's back.

He left the camp by the sundown light,
  And the settlers out on the Marthaguy
Awoke and heard, in the dead of night,
  A single horseman hurrying by.
He crossed the Bogan at Dandaloo,
  And many a mile of the silent plain
That lonely rider behind him threw
  Before they settled to sleep again.

He rode all night, and he steered his course
  By the shining stars with a bushman's skill,
And every time that he pressed his horse
  The Swagman answered him gamely still.
He neared his home as the east was bright.
  The doctor met him outside the town
"Carew! How far did you come last night?"
  "A hundred miles since the sun went down."

And his wife got round, and an oath he passed,
  So long as he or one of his breed
Could raise a coin, though it took their last,
  The Swagman never should want a feed.
And Kate Carew, when her father died,
  She kept the horse and she kept him well;
The pride of the district far and wide,
  He lived in style at the bush hotel.

Such was The Swagman; and Ryan knew
  Nothing about could pace the crack;
Little he'd care for the man in blue
  If once he got on The Swagman's back.
But how to do it? A word let fall
  Gave him the hint as the girl passed by;
Nothing but "Swagman—stable wall;
  Go to the stable and mind your eye."

He caught her meaning, and quickly turned
  To the trooper: "Reckon you'll gain a stripe
By arresting me, and it's easily earned;
  Let's go to the stable and get my pipe,
The Swagman has it." So off they went,
  And as soon as ever they turned their backs
The girl slipped down, on some errand bent
  Behind the stable and seized an axe.

The trooper stood at the stable door
    While Ryan went in quite cool and slow,
And then (the trick had been played before)
    The girl outside gave the wall a blow.
Three slabs fell out of the stable wall—
    'Twas done 'fore ever the trooper knew—
And Ryan, as soon as he saw them fall,
    Mounted The Swagman and rushed him through.

The trooper heard the hoof-beats ring
    In the stable yard, and he slammed the gate,
But The Swagman rose with a mighty spring
    At the fence, and the trooper fired too late
As they raced away, and his shots flew wide,
    And Ryan no longer need care a rap,
For never a horse that was lapped in hide
    Could catch The Swagman in Conroy's Gap.

And that's the story. You want to know
    If Ryan came back to his Kate Carew;
Of course he should have, as stories go,
    But the worst of it is this story's true:
And in real life it's a certain rule,
    Whatever poets and authors say
Of high-toned robbers and all their school,
    These horsethief fellows aren't built that way.

Come back! Don't hope it—the slinking hound,
    He sloped across to the Queensland side,
And sold The Swagman for fifty pound,
    And stole the money, and more beside.
And took to drink, and by some good chance
    Was killed—thrown out of a stolen trap.
And that was the end of this small romance,
    The end of the story of Conroy's Gap.

OUR
NEW HORSE

THE boys had come back from the races
  All silent and down on their luck;
They'd backed 'em, straight out and for places,
  But never a winner they struck.
They lost their good money on Slogan,
  And fell most uncommonly flat
When Partner, the pride of the Bogan,
  Was beaten by Aristocrat.

And one said, "I move that instanter
  We sell out our horses and quit;
The brutes ought to win in a canter,
  Such trials they do when they're fit.
The last one they ran was a snorter—
  A gallop to gladden one's heart—
Two-twelve for a mile and a quarter,
  And finished as straight as a dart.

"And then when I think that they're ready
  To win me a nice little swag,
They are licked like the veriest neddy—
  They're licked from the fall of the flag.
The mare held her own to the stable,
  She died out to nothing at that,
And Partner he never seemed able
  To pace with the Aristocrat.

"And times have been bad, and the seasons
  Don't promise to be of the best;
In short, boys, there's plenty of reasons
  For giving the racing a rest.
The mare can be kept on the station—
  Her breeding is good as can be—
But Partner, his next destination
  Is rather a trouble to me.

"We can't sell him here, for they know him
  As well as the clerk of the course;
He's raced and won races till, blow him,
  He's done as a handicap horse.

16

"Clancy rides behind them singing . . ."—
Norman Lindsay's frontispiece for *The Man from Snowy River*

A jady, uncertain performer,
  They weight him right out of the hunt,
And clap it on warmer and warmer
  Whenever he gets near the front.

"It's no use to paint him or dot him
  Or put any fake on his brand,
For bushmen are smart, and they'd spot him
  In any sale-yard in the land.
The folk about here could all tell him,
  Could swear to each separate hair;
Let us send him to Sydney and sell him,
  There's plenty of Jugginses there.

"We'll call him a maiden, and treat 'em
  To trials will open their eyes;
We'll run their best horses and beat 'em,
  And then won't they think him a prize.
I pity the fellow that buys him,
  He'll find in a very short space,
No matter how highly he tries him,
  The beggar won't *race* in a race."

          .   .   .   .   .

Next week, under "Seller and Buyer",
  Appeared in the *Daily Gazette*:
"A racehorse for sale, and a flyer;
  Has never been started as yet;
A trial will show what his pace is;
  The buyer can get him in light,
And win all the handicap races.
  Apply before Saturday night."

He sold for a hundred and thirty,
  Because of a gallop he had
One morning with Bluefish and Bertie.
  And donkey-licked both of 'em bad.
And when the old horse had departed,
  The life on the station grew tame;
The race-track was dull and deserted,
  The boys had gone back on the game.

          .   .   .   .   .

17

The winter rolled by, and the station
   Was green with the garland of Spring;
A spirit of glad exultation
   Awoke in each animate thing;
And all the old love, the old longing,
   Broke out in the breasts of the boys—
The visions of racing came thronging
   With all its delirious joys.

The rushing of floods in their courses,
   The rattle of rain on the roofs,
Recalled the fierce rush of the horses,
   The thunder of galloping hoofs.
And soon one broke out: "I can suffer
   No longer the life of a slug;
The man that don't race is a duffer,
   Let's have one more run for the mug.

"Why, everything races, no matter
   Whatever its method may be:
The waterfowl hold a regatta;
   The possums run heats up a tree;
The emus are constantly sprinting
   A handicap out on the plain;
It seems that all nature is hinting
   'Tis time to be at it again.

"The cockatoo parrots are talking
   Of races to far-away lands;
The native companions are walking
   A go-as-you-please on the sands;
The little foals gallop for pastime;
   The wallabies race down the gap;
Let's try it once more for the last time—
   Bring out the old jacket and cap.

"And now for a horse; we might try one
   Of those that are bred on the place.
But I fancy it's better to buy one,
   A horse that has proved he can race.
Let us send down to Sydney to Skinner,
   A thorough good judge who can ride,
And ask him to buy us a spinner
   To clean out the whole country-side."

They wrote him a letter as follows:
 "We want you to buy us a horse;
He must have the speed to catch swallows,
 And stamina with it, of course.
The price ain't a thing that'll grieve us,
 It's getting a bad un annoys
The undersigned blokes, and believe us,
 We're yours to a cinder, 'the boys'."

He answered: "I've bought you a hummer,
 A horse that has never been raced;
I saw him run over The Drummer,
 He held him outclassed and outpaced.
His breeding's not known, but they state he
 Is born of a thoroughbred strain.
I've paid them a hundred and eighty,
 And started the horse in the train."

They met him—alas, that these verses
 Aren't up to the subject's demands,
Can't set forth their eloquent curses—
 For Partner was back on their hands.
They went in to meet him in gladness,
 They opened his box with delight—
A silent procession of sadness
 They crept to the station at night.

And life has grown dull on the station,
 The boys are all silent and slow;
Their work is a daily vexation,
 And sport is unknown to them now.
Whenever they think how they stranded,
 They squeal just as guinea-pigs squeal;
They'd bit their own hook, and were landed
 With fifty pounds loss on the deal.

AN IDYLL
OF DANDALOO

On Western plains, where shade is not,
   'Neath summer skies of cloudless blue,
Where all is dry and all is hot,
   There stands the town of Dandaloo—
A township where life's total sum
Is sleep, diversified with rum.

Its grass-grown streets with dust are deep,
   'Twere vain endeavour to express
The dreamless silence of its sleep,
   Its wide, expansive drunkenness.
The yearly races mostly drew
A lively crowd at Dandaloo.

There came a sportsman from the East,
   The eastern land where sportsmen blow,
And brought with him a speedy beast—
   A speedy beast as horses go.
He came afar in hope to "do"
The little town of Dandaloo.

Now this was weak of him, I wot—
   Exceeding weak, it seemed to me—
For we in Dandaloo were not
   The Jugginses we seemed to be;
In fact, we rather thought we knew
Our book by heart in Dandaloo.

We held a meeting at the bar,
   And met the question fair and square—
"We've stumped the country near and far
   To raise the cash for races here;
We've got a hundred pounds or two—
Not half so bad for Dandaloo.

"And now, it seems we have to be
   Cleaned out by this here Sydney bloke,
With his imported horse; and he
   Will scoop the pool and leave us broke.
Shall we sit still, and make no fuss
While this chap climbs all over us?"

   .   .   .   .   .

The races came to Dandaloo,
  And all the cornstalks from the West
On every kind of moke and screw
  Come forth in all their glory drest.
The stranger's horse, as hard as nails,
Look'd fit to run for New South Wales.

He won the race by half a length—
  Quite half a length, it seemed to me—
But Dandaloo, with all its strength,
  Roared out "Dead heat!" most fervently;
And, after hesitation meet,
The judge's verdict was "Dead heat!"

And many men there were could tell
  What gave the verdict extra force.
The stewards—and the judge as well—
  They all had backed the second horse.
For things like this they sometimes do
In larger towns than Dandaloo.

They ran it off, the stranger won,
  Hands down, by near a hundred yards.
He smiled to think his troubles done;
  But Dandaloo held all the cards.
They went to scale and—cruel fate!—
His jockey turned out under weight.

Perhaps they'd tampered with the scale!
  I cannot tell. I only know
It weighed him out all right. I fail
  To paint that Sydney sportsman's woe.
He said the stewards were a crew
Of low-lived thieves in Dandaloo.

He lifted up his voice, irate,
  And swore till all the air was blue;
So then we rose to vindicate
  The dignity of Dandaloo.
"Look here," said we, "you must not poke
Such oaths at us poor country folk."

We rode him softly on a rail,
　　We shied at him, in careless glee,
Some large tomatoes, rank and stale,
　　And eggs of great antiquity—
Their wild, unholy fragrance flew
About the town of Dandaloo.

He left the town at break of day,
　　He led his racehorse through the streets,
And now he tells the tale, they say,
　　To every racing man he meets.
And Sydney sportsmen all eschew
The atmosphere of Dandaloo.

THE GEEBUNG
POLO CLUB

IT was somewhere up the country, in a land of rock and scrub,
That they formed an institution called the Geebung Polo Club.
They were long and wiry natives from the rugged mountain side,
And the horse was never saddled that the Geebungs couldn't ride;
But their style of playing polo was irregular and rash—
They had mighty little science, but a mighty lot of dash:
And they played on mountain ponies that were muscular and
     strong,
Though their coats were quite unpolished, and their manes and tails
     were long.
And they used the train those ponies wheeling cattle in the scrub;
They were demons, were the members of the Geebung Polo Club.

It was somewhere down the country, in a city's smoke and steam,
That a polo club existed, called "The Cuff and Collar Team".
As a social institution 'twas a marvellous success,
For the members were distinguished by exclusiveness and dress.
They had natty little ponies that were nice, and smooth, and sleek,
For their cultivated owners only rode 'em once a week.
So they started up the country in pursuit of sport and fame,
For they meant to show the Geebungs how they ought to play
     the game;
And they took their valets with them—just to give their boots
     a rub
Ere they started operations on the Geebung Polo Club.

Now my readers can imagine how the contest ebbed and flowed,
When the Geebung boys got going it was time to clear the road;
And the game was so terrific that ere half the time was gone
A spectator's leg was broken—just from merely looking on.
For they waddied one another till the plain was strewn with dead,
While the score was kept so even that they neither got ahead.
And the Cuff and Collar Captain, when he tumbled off to die
Was the last surviving player—so the game was called a tie.

Then the Captain of the Geebungs raised him slowly from the
     ground,
Though his wounds were mostly mortal, yet he fiercely gazed
     around;

There was no one to oppose him—all the rest were in a trance,
So he scrambled on his pony for his last expiring chance,
For he meant to make an effort to get victory to his side;
So he struck at goal—and missed it—then he tumbled off and died.

. . . .

By the old Campaspe River, where the breezes shake the grass,
There's a row of little gravestones that the stockmen never pass,
For they bear a rude inscription saying, "Stranger, drop a tear,
For the Cuff and Collar players and the Geebung boys lie here."
And on misty moonlit evenings, while the dingoes howl around,
You can see their shadows flitting down that phantom polo ground;
You can hear the loud collisions as the flying players meet,
And the rattle of the mallets, and the rush of ponies' feet,
Till the terrified spectator rides like blazes to the pub—
He's been haunted by the spectres of the Geebung Polo Club.

THE TRAVELLING
POST OFFICE

THE roving breezes come and go, the reed-beds sweep and sway,
The sleepy river murmurs low, and loiters on its way,
It is the land of lots o' time along the Castlereagh.

    .   .   .   .   .

The old man's son had left the farm, he found it dull and slow,
He drifted to the great North-west, where all the rovers go.
"He's gone so long," the old man said, "he's dropped right out
    of mind,
But if you'd write a line to him I'd take it very kind;
He's shearing here and fencing there, a kind of waif and stray—
He's droving now with Conroy's sheep along the Castlereagh.

"The sheep are travelling for the grass, and travelling very slow;
They may be at Mundooran now, or past the Overflow,
Or tramping down the black-soil flats across by Waddiwong
But all those little country towns would send the letter wrong.
The mailman, if he's extra tired, would pass them in his sleep;
It's safest to address the note to 'Care of Conroy's sheep',
For five and twenty thousand head can scarcely go astray,
You write to 'Care of Conroy's sheep along the Castlereagh'."

    .   .   .   .   .

By rock and ridge and riverside the western mail has gone
Across the great Blue Mountain Range to take that letter on.
A moment on the topmost grade, while open fire-doors glare,
She pauses like a living thing to breathe the mountain air,
Then launches down the other side across the plains away
To bear that note to "Conroy's sheep along the Castlereagh".

And now by coach and mailman's bag it goes from town to town,
And Conroy's Gap and Conroy's Creek have marked it "Further
    down".
Beneath a sky of deepest blue, where never cloud abides,
A speck upon the waste of plain the lonely mailman rides.
Where fierce hot winds have set the pine and myall boughs
    asweep
He hails the shearers passing by for news of Conroy's sheep.
By big lagoons where wildfowl play and crested pigeons flock,
By camp-fires where the drovers ride around their restless stock,
And past the teamster toiling down to fetch the wool away
My letter chases Conroy's sheep along the Castlereagh.

SALTBUSH BILL

Now this is the law of the Overland that all in the West obey—
A man must cover with travelling sheep a six-mile stage a day;
But this is the law which the drovers make, right easily understood,
They travel their stage where the grass is bad, but they camp
  where the grass is good;
They camp, and they ravage the squatter's grass till never a
  blade remains.
Then they drift away as the white clouds drift on the edge of the
  saltbush plains:
From camp to camp and from run to run they battle it hand to
  hand
For a blade of grass and the right to pass on the track of the
  Overland.
For this is the law of the Great Stock Routes, 'tis written in
  white and black—
The man that goes with a travelling mob must keep to a half-mile
  track;
And the drovers keep to a half-mile track on the runs where the
  grass is dead,
But they spread their sheep on a well-grassed run till they go
  with a two-mile spread.
So the squatters hurry the drovers on from dawn till the fall of
  night,
And the squatters' dogs and the drovers' dogs get mixed in a
  deadly fight.
Yet the squatters' men, though they haunt the mob, are willing
  the peace to keep,
For the drovers learn how to use their hands when they go with
  the travelling sheep;
But this is the tale of a Jackeroo that came from a foreign strand,
And the fight that he fought with Saltbush Bill, the King of
  the Overland.

Now Saltbush Bill was a drover tough as ever the country knew,
He had fought his way on the Great Stock Routes from the sea
  to the big Barcoo;
He could tell when he came to a friendly run that gave him a
  chance to spread,

And he knew where the hungry owners were that hurried his
    sheep ahead;
He was drifting down in the Eighty drought with a mob that
    could scarcely creep
(When the kangaroos by the thousand starve, it is rough on the
    travelling sheep),
And he camped one night at the crossing-place on the edge of
    the Wilga run;
"We must manage a feed for them here," he said, "or half of the
    mob are done!"
So he spread them out when they left the camp wherever they
    liked to go,
Till he grew aware of a Jackaroo with a station-hand in tow.

They set to work on the straggling sheep, and with many a
    stockwhip crack
They forced them in where the grass was dead in the space of
    the half-mile track;
And William prayed that the hand of Fate might suddenly strike
    him blue
But he'd get some grass for his starving sheep in the teeth of that
    Jackaroo.
So he turned and he cursed the Jackaroo; he cursed him, alive
    or dead,
From the soles of his great unwieldly feet to the crown of his
    ugly head,
With an extra curse on the moke he rode and the cur at his
    heels that ran,
Till the Jackaroo from his horse got down and went for the
    drover-man;
With the station-hand for his picker-up, though the sheep ran
    loose the while,
They battled it out on the well-grassed plain in the regular prize-
    ring style.

Now, the new chum fought for his honour's sake and the pride
    of the English race,
But the drover fought for his daily bread with a smile on his
    bearded face;
So he shifted ground, and he sparred for wind, and he made it
    a lengthy mill,
And from time to time as his scouts came in they whispered to
    Saltbush Bill—

"We have spread the sheep with a two-mile spread, and the grass
    it is something grand;
You must stick to him, Bill, for another round for the pride of
    the Overland."
The new chum made it a rushing fight, though never a blow
    got home,
Till the sun rode high in the cloudless sky and glared on the
    brick-red loam,
Till the sheep drew in to the shelter-trees and settled them down
    to rest;
Then the drover said he would fight no more, and gave his
    opponent best.

So the new chum rode to the homestead straight, and told them a
    story grand
Of the desperate fight that he fought that day with the King
    of the Overland;
And the tale went home to the Public Schools of the pluck of the
    English swell—
How the drover fought for his very life, but blood in the end
    must tell.
But the travelling sheep and the Wilga sheep were boxed on the
    Old Man Plain;
'Twas a full week's work ere they drafted out and hunted them
    off again;
A week's good grass in their wretched hides, with a curse and a
    stockwhip crack
They hunted them off on the road once more to starve on the
    half-mile track.
And Saltbush Bill, on the Overland, will many a time recite
How the best day's work that he ever did was the day that he
    lost the fight.

A MOUNTAIN STATION

I BOUGHT a run a while ago
  On country rough and ridgy,
Where wallaroos and wombats grow—
  The Upper Murrumbidgee.
The grass is rather scant, it's true,
  But this a fair exchange is,
The sheep can see a lovely view
  By climbing up the ranges.

And She-oak Flat's the station's name,
  I'm not surprised at that, sirs:
The oaks were there before I came,
  And I supplied the flat, sirs.
A man would wonder how it's done,
  The stock so soon decreases—
They sometimes tumble off the run
  And break themselves to pieces.

I've tried to make expenses meet,
  But wasted all my labours;
The sheep the dingoes didn't eat
  Were stolen by the neighbours.
They stole my pears—my native pears—
  Those thrice-convicted felons,
And ravished from me unawares
  My crop of paddy-melons.

And sometimes under sunny skies,
  Without an explanation,
The Murrumbidgee used to rise
  And overflow the station.
But this was caused (as now I know)
  When summer sunshine glowing
Had melted all Kiandra's snow
  And set the river going.

Then in the news, perhaps, you read:
　"Stock Passings. Puckawidgee,
Fat cattle: Seven hundred head
　Swept down the Murrumbidgee;
Their destination's quite obscure,
　But, somehow, there's a notion,
Unless the river falls, they're sure
　To reach the Southern Ocean."

So after that I'll give it best;
　No more with Fate I'll battle.
I'll let the river take the rest,
　For those were all my cattle.
And with one comprehensive curse
　I close my brief narration,
And advertise it in my verse—
　"For Sale! A Mountain Station."

BEEN THERE BEFORE

THERE came a stranger to Walgett town,
  To Walgett town when the sun was low,
And he carried a thirst that was worth a crown,
  Yet how to quench it he did not know;
But he thought he might take those yokels down,
The guileless yokels of Walgett town.

They made him a bet in a private bar,
  In a private bar when the talk was high,
And they bet him some pounds no matter how far
  He could pelt a stone, yet he could not shy
A stone right over the river so brown,
The Darling River at Walgett town.

He knew that the river from bank to bank
  Was fifty yards, and he smiled a smile
As he trundled down; but his hopes they sank,
  For there wasn't a stone within fifty mile;
For the saltbush plain and the open down
Produce no quarries in Walgett town.

The yokels laughed at his hopes o'erthrown,
  And he stood awhile like a man in a dream;
Then he out of his pocket he fetched a stone,
  And pelted it over the silent stream—
He'd been there before; he had wandered down
On a previous visit to Walgett town.

THE MAN WHO
WAS AWAY

THE widow sought the lawyer's room with children three in tow,
She told the lawyer man her tale in tones of deepest woe.
She said, "My husband took to drink for pains in his inside,
And never drew a sober breath from then until he died.

"He never drew a sober breath, he died without a will,
And I must sell the bit of land the childer's mouths to fill.
There's some is grown and gone away, but some is childer yet,
And times is very bad indeed—a livin's hard to get.

"There's Min and Sis and little Chris, they stops at home with me,
And Sal has married Greenhide Bill that breaks for Bidgeree.
And Fred is drovin' Conroy's sheep along the Castlereagh
And Charley's shearin' down the Bland, and Peter is away."

The lawyer wrote the details down in ink of legal blue—
"There's Minnie, Susan, Christopher, they stop at home with you;
There's Sarah, Frederick, and Charles, I'll write to them today,
But what about the other son—the one who is away?

"You'll have to furnish his consent to sell the bit of land."
The widow shuffled in her seat, "Oh, don't you understand?
I thought a lawyer ought to know—I don't know what to say—
You'll have to do without him, boss, for Peter is away."

But here the little boy spoke up—said he, "We thought you knew;
He's done six months in Goulburn gaol—he's got six more to do."
Thus in one comprehensive flash he made it clear as day,
The mystery of Peter's life—the man who was away.

THE MAN
FROM IRONBARK

It was the man from Ironbark who struck the Sydney town,
He wandered over street and park, he wandered up and down.
He loitered here, he loitered there, till he was like to drop,
Until at last in sheer despair he sought a barber's shop.
"'Ere! shave my beard and whiskers off, I'll be a man of mark,
I'll go and do the Sydney toff up home in Ironbark."

The barber man was small and flash, as barbers mostly are,
He wore a strike-your-fancy sash, he smoked a huge cigar:
He was a humorist of note and keen at repartee,
He laid the odds and kept a "tote", whatever that may be.
And when he saw our friend arrive, he whispered "Here's a lark!
Just watch me catch him all alive this man from Ironbark."

There were some gilded youths that sat along the barber's wall,
Their eyes were dull, their heads were flat, they had no brains
        at all;
To them the barber passed the wink, his dexter eyelid shut,
"I'll make this bloomin' yokel think his bloomin' throat is cut."
And as he soaped and rubbed it in he made a rude remark:
"I s'pose the flats is pretty green up there in Ironbark."

A grunt was all reply he got; he shaved the bushman's chin,
Then made the water boiling hot and dipped the razor in.
He raised his hand, his brow grew black, he paused awhile to
        gloat,
Then slashed the red-hot razor-back across his victim's throat;
Upon the newly-shaven skin it made a livid mark—
No doubt it fairly took him in—the man from Ironbark.

He fetched a wild up-country yell might wake the dead to hear,
And though his throat, he knew full well, was cut from ear to ear,
He struggled gamely to his feet, and faced the murderous foe.
"You've done for me! you dog, I'm beat! one hit before I go!
I only wish I had a knife, you blessed murdering shark!
But you'll remember all your life the man from Ironbark."

He lifted up his hairy paw, with one tremendous clout
He landed on the barber's jaw, and knocked the barber out.
He set to work with tooth and nail, he made the place a wreck;
He grabbed the nearest gilded youth, and tried to break his neck.
And all the while his throat he held to save his vital spark,
And "Murder! Bloody Murder!" yelled the man from Ironbark.

A peeler man who heard the din came in to see the show;
He tried to run the bushman in, but he refused to go.
And when at last the barber spoke, and said " 'Twas all in fun—
'Twas just a little harmless joke, a trifle overdone."
"A joke!" he cried, "By George, that's fine; a lively sort of lark;
I'd like to catch that murdering swine some night in Ironbark."

And now while round the shearing-floor the listening shearers gape,
He tells the story o'er and o'er, and brags of his escape.
"Them barber chaps what keeps a tote, by George, I've had enough,
One tried to cut my bloomin' throat, but thank the Lord it's tough."
And whether he's believed or no, there's one thing to remark,
That flowing beards are all the go way up in Ironbark.

THE OPEN STEEPLECHASE

I HAD ridden over hurdles up the country once or twice,
By the side of Snowy River with a horse they called "The Ace".
And we brought him down to Sydney, and our rider, Jimmy Rice,
Got a fall and broke his shoulder, so they nabbed me in a trice—
Me, that never wore the colours, for the Open Steeplechase.

"Make the running," said the trainer, "it's your only chance
    whatever,
Make it hot from start to finish, for the old black horse can stay,
And just think of how they'll take it, when they hear on Snowy
    River
That the country boy was plucky, and the country horse was
    clever.
You must ride for old Monaro and the mountain boys today."

"Are you ready?" said the starter, as we held the horses back.
All ablazing with impatience, with excitement all aglow;
Before us like a ribbon stretched the steeplechasing track,
And the sun-rays glistened brightly on the chestnut and the black
As the starter's words came slowly, "Are—you—ready? Go!"

Well I scarcely knew we'd started, I was stupid-like with wonder
Till the field closed up beside me and a jump appeared ahead.
And we flew it like a hurdle, not a baulk and not a blunder,
As we charged it all together, and it fairly whistled under,
And then some were pulled behind me and a few shot out and led.

So we ran for half the distance, and I'm making no pretences
When I tell you I was feeling very nervous-like and queer,
For those jockeys rode like demons; you would think they'd lost
    their senses
If you saw them rush their horses at those rasping five-foot fences—
And in place of making running I was falling to the rear.

Till a chap came racing past me on a horse they called "The
    Quiver",
And said he, "My country joker, are you going to give it best?
Are you frightened of the fences? does their stoutness make you
    shiver?
Have they come to breeding cowards by the side of Snowy River?
Are there riders on Monaro?——" but I never heard the rest.

For I drove The Ace and sent him just as fast as he could pace it
At the big black line of timber stretching fair across the track,
And he shot beside The Quiver. "Now," said I, "my boy, we'll
    race it.
You can come with Snowy River if you're only game to face it,
Let us mend the pace a little and we'll see who cries a crack."

So we raced away together, and we left the others standing,
And the people cheered and shouted as we settled down to ride,
And we clung beside The Quiver. At his taking off and landing
I could see his scarlet nostril and his mighty ribs expanding,
And The Ace stretched out in earnest, and we held him stride
    for stride.

But the pace was so terrific that they soon ran out their tether—
They were rolling in their gallop, they were fairly blown and
    beat—
But they both were game as pebbles—neither one would show the
    feather.
And we rushed them at the fences, and they cleared them both
    together,
Nearly every time they clouted, but they somehow kept their feet.

Then the last jump rose before us, and they faced it game as
    ever—
We were both at spur and whipcord, fetching blood at every
    bound—
And above the people's cheering and the cries of "Ace" and "Quiver",
I could hear the trainer shouting, "One more run for Snowy River."
Then we struck the jump together and came smashing to the
    ground.

Well, The Quiver ran to blazes, but The Ace stood still and
    waited,
Stood and waited like a statue while I scrambled on his back.
There was no one next or near me for the field was fairly slated,
So I cantered home a winner with my shoulder dislocated,
While the man who rode The Quiver followed limping down the
    track.

And he shook my hand and told me that in all his days he never
Met a man who rode more gamely, and our last set-to was prime.
Then we wired them on Monaro how we chanced to beat The
      Quiver,
And they sent us back an answer, "Good old sort from Snowy
      River:
Send us word each race you start in and we'll back you every
      time."

THE
AMATEUR RIDER

Hɪᴍ going to ride for us! *Him*—with the pants and the eyeglass
    and all.
Amateur! don't he just look it—it's twenty to one on a fall.
Boss must be gone off his head to be sending our steeplechase
    crack
Out over fences like these with an object like that on his back.

Ride! Don't tell *me* he can ride. With his pants just as loose
    as balloons,
How can he sit on a horse? and his spurs like a pair of harpoons;
Ought to be under the Dog Act, he ought, and be kept off the
    course.
Fall! why, he'd fall off a cart, let alone off a steeplechase horse.

.   .   .   .

Yessir! the 'orse is all ready—I wish you'd have rode him before;
Nothing like knowing your 'orse, sir, and this chap's a terror
    to bore;
Battleaxe always could pull, and he rushes his fences like fun—
Stands off his jump twenty feet, and then springs like a shot
    from a gun.

Oh, he can jump 'em all right, sir, you make no mistake, 'e's a toff—
Clouts 'em in earnest, too, sometimes; you mind that he don't
    clout you off—
Don't seem to mind how he hits 'em, his shins is as hard as a nail,
Sometimes you'll see the fence shake and the splinters fly up
    from the rail.

All you can do is to hold him and just let him jump as he likes,
Give him his head at the fences, and hang on like death if he
    strikes;
Don't let him run himself out—you can lie third or fourth in
    the race—
Until you clear the stone wall, and from that you can put on
    the pace.

Fell at that wall once, he did, and it gave him a regular spread,
Ever since that time he flies it—he'll stop if you pull at his head,
Just let him race—you can trust him—he'll take first-class care
    he don't fall,
And I think that's the lot—but remember, he must have his head
    at the wall.

      .   .   .   .

Well, he's down safe as far as the start, and he seems to sit on
    pretty neat,
Only his baggified breeches would ruinate anyone's seat—
They're away—here they come—the first fence, and he's head over
    heels for a crown!
Good for the new chum, he's over, and two of the others are
    down!

Now for the treble, my hearty—By Jove, he can ride, after all;
Whoop, that's your sort—let him fly them! He hasn't much fear
    of a fall.
Who in the world would have thought it? And aren't they just going
    a pace?
Little Recruit in the lead there will make it a stoutly-run race.

Lord! but they're racing in earnest—and down goes Recruit on
    his head,
Rolling clean over his boy—it's a miracle if he ain't dead.
Battleaxe, Battleaxe, yet! By the Lord, he's got most of 'em beat—
Ho! did you see how he struck, and the swell never moved in
    his seat?

Second time round, and, by Jingo! he's holding his lead of 'em well;
Hark to him clouting the timber! It don't seem to trouble the swell.
Now for the wall—let him rush it. A thirty-foot leap, I declare—
Never a shift in his seat, and he's racing for home like a hare.

What's that that's chasing him—Rataplan—regular demon to stay!
Sit down and ride for your life now! Oh, good, that's the style—
    come away!
Rataplan's certain to beat you, unless you can give him the slip,
Sit down and rub in the whalebone—now give him the spurs and
    the whip!

Battleaxe, Battleaxe, yet—and it's Battleaxe wins for a crown;
Look at him rushing the fences, he wants to bring t'other chap
    down.
Rataplan never will catch him if only he keeps on his pins;
Now! the last fence, and he's over it! Battleaxe, Battleaxe wins!

    .   .   .   .

Well, sir, you rode him just perfect—I knew from the fust you
    could ride.
Some of the chaps said you couldn't, an' I says just like this a'
    one side:
Mark me, I says, that's a tradesman—the saddle is where he was bred.
Weight! you're all right, sir, and thank you; and them was the
    words that I said.

ON
KILEY'S RUN

THE roving breezes come and go
                   On Kiley's Run,
The sleepy river murmurs low,
And far away one dimly sees
Beyond the stretch of forest trees—
Beyond the foothills dusk and dun—
The ranges steeping in the sun
                   On Kiley's Run.

'Tis many years since first I came
                   To Kiley's Run,
More years than I would care to name
Since I, a stripling, used to ride
For miles and miles at Kiley's side,
The while in stirring tones he told
The stories of the days of old
                   On Kiley's Run.

I see the old bush homestead now
                   On Kiley's Run,
Just nestled down beneath the brow
Of one small ridge above the sweep
Of river-flat, where willows weep
And jasmine flowers and roses bloom:
The air was laden with perfume
                   On Kiley's Run.

We lived the good old station life
                   On Kiley's Run,
With little thought of care or strife.
Old Kiley seldom used to roam,
He liked to make the Run his home;
The swagmen never turned away
With empty hand at close of day
                   From Kiley's Run.

We kept a racehorse now and then
                    On Kiley's Run,
And neighbouring stations brought their men
To meetings where the sport was free,
And dainty ladies came to see
Their champions ride; with laugh and song
The old house rang the whole night long
                    On Kiley's Run.

The station-hands were friends, I wot,
                    On Kiley's Run,
A reckless, merry-hearted lot—
All splendid riders, and they knew
The boss was kindness through and through.
Old Kiley always stood their friend,
And so they served him to the end
                    On Kiley's Run.

But droughts and losses came apace
                    To Kiley's Run,
Till ruin stared him in the face;
He toiled and toiled while lived the light,
He dreamed of overdrafts at night:
At length, because he could not pay,
His bankers took the stock away
                    From Kiley's Run.

Old Kiley stood and saw them go
                    From Kiley's Run.
The well-bred cattle marching slow;
His stockmen, mates for many a day,
They wrung his hand and went away.
Too old to make another start,
Old Kiley died—of broken heart,
                    On Kiley's Run.

The owner lives in England now
                    Of Kiley's Run.
He knows a racehorse from a cow;
But that is all he knows of stock:
His chiefest care is how to dock
Expenses, and he sends from town
To cut the shearers' wages down
                    On Kiley's Run.

There are no neighbours anywhere
                    Near Kiley's Run.
The hospitable homes are bare,
The gardens gone; for no pretence
Must hinder cutting down expense;
The homestead that we held so dear
Contains a half-paid overseer
                    On Kiley's Run.

All life and sport and hope have died
                    On Kiley's Run.
No longer there the stockmen ride;
For sour-faced boundary riders creep
On mongrel horses after sheep,
Through ranges where, at racing speed,
Old Kiley used to "wheel the lead"
                    On Kiley's Run.

There runs a lane for thirty miles
                    Through Kiley's Run.
On either side the herbage smiles,
But wretched travelling sheep must pass
Without a drink or blade of grass
Through that long lane of death and shame:
The weary drovers curse the name
                    Of Kiley's Run.

The name itself is changed of late
                    Of Kiley's Run.
They call it "Chandos Park Estate".
The lonely swagman through the dark
Must hump his swag past Chandos Park—
The name is English, don't you see;
The old name sweeter sounds to me
                    Of Kiley's Run.

I cannot guess what fate will bring
                    To Kiley's Run—
For chances come and changes ring—
I scarcely think 'twill always be
Locked up to suit an absentee;
And if he lets it out in farms
His tenants soon will carry arms
                    On Kiley's Run.

FRYING PAN'S THEOLOGY

SCENE: On Monaro.
Dramatis Personae
Shock-headed blackfellow,
   Boy (on a pony).

Snowflakes are falling
   Gentle and slow,
Youngster says, "Frying Pan
   What makes it snow?"

Frying Pan, confident,
   Makes the reply—
"Shake 'im big flour bag
   Up in the sky!"

"What! when there's miles of it?
   Surely that's brag.
Who is there strong enough
   Shake such a bag?"

"What parson tellin' you,
   Ole Mister Dodd,
Tell you in Sunday-school?
   Big pfeller God!

"Him drive 'im bullock dray,
   Then thunder go;
Him shake 'im flour bag—
   Tumble down snow!"

THE TWO
DEVINES

It was shearing-time at the Myall Lake,
   And then rose the sound through the livelong day
Of the constant clash that the shear-blades make
   When the fastest shearers are making play;
But there wasn't a man in the shearers' lines
That could shear a sheep with the two Devines.

They had rung the sheds of the east and west,
   Had beaten the cracks of the Walgett side,
And the Cooma shearers had given them best—
   When they saw them shear, they were satisfied.
From the southern slopes to the western pines
They were noted men, were the two Devines.

Twas a wether flock that had come to hand,
   Great struggling brutes, that shearers shirk,
For the fleece was filled with the grass and sand,
   And seventy sheep was a big day's work.
"At a pound a hundred it's dashed hard lines
To shear such sheep," said the two Devines.

But the shearers knew that they'd make a cheque
   When they came to deal with the station ewes;
They were bare of belly and bare of neck
   With a fleece as light as a kangaroo's.
"We will show the boss how a shear-blade shines
When we reach those ewes," said the two Devines.

But it chanced next day, when the stunted pines
   Were swayed and stirred by the dawn-wind's breath,
That a message came for the two Devines
   That their father lay at the point of death.
So away at speed through the whispering pines
Down the bridle-track rode the two Devines.

It was fifty miles to their father's hut,
   And the dawn was bright when they rode away;
At the fall of night, when the shed was shut
   And the men had rest from the toilsome day,
To the shed once more through the darkening pines
On their weary steeds came the two Devines.

"Well, you're back right sudden," the super said;
  "Is the old man dead and the funeral done?"
"Well, no sir, he ain't not exactly dead,
  But as good as dead," said the eldest son—
"And we couldn't bear such a chance to lose,
So we came straight back to tackle the ewes."

     ·   ·   ·   ·   ·

They are shearing ewes at the Myall Lake,
  And the shed is merry the livelong day
With the clashing sound that the shear-blades make
  When the fastest shearers are making play;
And a couple of "hundred and ninety-nines"
Are the tallies made by the two Devines.

IN THE
DROVING DAYS

"ONLY a pound," said the auctioneer,
"Only a pound; and I'm standing here
Selling this animal, gain or loss—
Only a pound for the drover's horse?
One of the sort that was ne'er afraid,
One of the boys of the Old Brigade;
Thoroughly honest and game, I'll swear,
Only a little the worse for wear;
Plenty as bad to be seen in town,
Give me a bid and I'll knock him down;
Sold as he stands, and without recourse,
Give me a bid for the drover's horse."

Loitering there in an aimless way
Somehow I noticed the poor old grey,
Weary and battered and screwed, of course;
Yet when I noticed the old grey horse,
The rough bush saddle, and single rein
Of the bridle laid on his tangled mane,
Straightway the crowd and the auctioneer
Seemed on a sudden to disappear,
Melted away in a kind of haze—
For my heart went back to the droving days.

Back to the road, and I crossed again
Over the miles of the saltbush plain—
The shining plain that is said to be
The dried-up bed of an inland sea.
Where the air so dry and so clear and bright
Refracts the sun with a wondrous light,
And out in the dim horizon makes
The deep blue gleam of the phantom lakes.

At dawn of day we could feel the breeze
That stirred the boughs of the sleeping trees,
And brought a breath of the fragrance rare
That comes and goes in that scented air;
For the trees and grass and the shrubs contain

A dry sweet scent on the saltbush plain.
For those that love it and understand
The saltbush plain is a wonderland,
A wondrous country, were Nature's ways
Were revealed to me in the droving days.

We saw the fleet wild horses pass,
And kangaroos through the Mitchell grass;
The emu ran with her frightened brood
All unmolested and unpursued.
But there rose a shout and a wild hubbub
When the dingo raced for his native scrub,
And he paid right dear for his stolen meals
With the drovers' dogs at his wretched heels.
For we ran him down at a rattling pace,
While the pack-horse joined in the stirring chase.
And a wild halloo at the kill we'd raise—
We were light of heart in the droving days.

'Twas a drover's horse, and my hand again
Made a move to close on a fancied rein.
For I felt the swing and the easy stride
Of the grand old horse that I used to ride.
In drought or plenty, in good or ill,
The same old steed was my comrade still;
The old grey horse with his honest ways
Was a mate to me in the droving days.

When we kept our watch in the cold and damp,
If the cattle broke from the sleeping camp,
Over the flats and across the plain,
With my head bent down on his waving mane,
Through the boughs above and the stumps below,
On the darkest night I could let him go
At a racing speed; he would choose his course,
And my life was safe with the old grey horse.
But man and horse had a favourite job,
When an outlaw broke from a station mob;
With a right good will was the stockwhip plied,
As the old horse raced at the straggler's side,
And the greenhide whip such a weal would raise—
We could use the whip in the droving days.

    ·   ·   ·   ·   ·

"Only a pound!" and was this the end—
Only a pound for the drover's friend.
The drover's friend that has seen his day,
And now was worthless and cast away
With a broken knee and a broken heart
To be flogged and starved in a hawker's cart.
Well, I made a bid for a sense of shame
And the memories dear of the good old game.

"Thank you? Guinea! and cheap at that!
Against you there in the curly hat!
Only a guinea, and one more chance,
Down he goes if there's no advance,
Third, and the last time, one! two! three!"
And the old grey horse was knocked down to me.
And now he's wandering, fat and sleek,
On the lucerne flats by the Homestead Creek;
I dare not ride him for fear he'd fall,
But he does a journey to beat them all,
For though he scarcely a trot can raise,
He can take me back to the droving days.

LOST

"HE ought to be home," said the old man. "without there's some-
    thing amiss.
He only went to the Two-mile—he ought to be back by this.
He *would* ride the Reckless filly, he *would* have his wilful way;
And here, he's not back at sundown—and what will his mother
    say?

"He was always his mother's idol, since ever his father died;
And there isn't a horse on the station that he isn't game to ride.
But that Reckless mare is vicious, and if once she gets away
He hasn't got strength to hold her—and what will his mother say?"

The old man walked to the sliprail, and peered up the darkening
    track,
And looked and longed for the rider that would never more come
    back;
And the mother came and clutched him, with sudden, spasmodic
    fright:
"What has become of my Willie?—why isn't he home tonight?"

Away in the gloomy ranges, at the foot of an ironbark,
The bonnie, winsome laddie was lying stiff and stark;
For the Reckless mare had smashed him against a leaning limb,
And his comely face was battered, and his merry eyes were dim.

And the thoroughbred chestnut filly, the saddle beneath her flanks,
Was away like fire through the ranges to join the wild mob's ranks;
And a broken-hearted woman and an old man worn and white
Were searching all day in the ranges till the sundown brought the
    night.

And the mother kept feebly calling, with a hope that would not die,
"Willie! where are you, Willie?" But how can the dead reply?
And hope died out with the daylight, and the darkness brought
    despair.
God pity the stricken mother, and answer the widow's prayer!

Though far and wide they sought him, they found not where he fell;
For the ranges held him precious, and guarded their treasure well.
The wattle blooms above him, and the blue bells blow close by,
And the brown bees buzz the secret, and the wild birds sing reply.

But the mother pined and faded, and cried, and took no rest,
And rode each day to the ranges on her hopeless, weary quest,
Seeking her loved one ever, she faded and pined away,
But with strength of her great affection she still sought every day.

"I know that sooner or later I shall find my boy," she said.
But she came not home one evening, and they found her lying dead,
And stamped on the poor pale features, as the spirit homeward
    passed,
Was an angel smile of gladness—she had found her boy at last.

OVER
THE RANGE

LITTLE bush maiden, wondering-eyed,
   Playing alone in the creek-bed dry,
In the small green flat on every side
   Walled in by the Moonbi ranges high;
Tell me the tale of your lonely life
   'Mid the great grey forests that know no change.
"I never have left my home," she said,
   "I have never been over the Moonbi Range.

"Father and mother are both long dead,
   And I live with granny in yon wee place."
"Where are your father and mother?" I said.
   She puzzled awhile with thoughtful face,
Then a light came into the shy brown eye,
   And she smiled, for she thought the question strange
On a thing so certain—"When people die
   They go to the country over the range."

"And what is this country like, my lass?"
   "There are blossoming trees and pretty flowers,
And shining creeks where the golden grass
   Is fresh and sweet from the summer showers.
They never need work, nor want, nor weep;
   No troubles can come their hearts to estrange.
Some summer night I shall fall asleep,
   And wake in the country over the range."

Child, you are wise in your simple trust,
   For the wisest man knows no more than you.
Ashes to ashes, and dust to dust:
   Our views by a range are bounded too;
But we know that God hath this gift in store,
   That, when we come to the final change,
We shall meet with our loved ones gone before
   To the beautiful country over the range.

ONLY
A JOCKEY

"Richard Bennison, a jockey, aged fourteen, while riding William Tell in his training, was thrown and killed. The horse is luckily uninjured."—Melbourne Wire.

Out in the grey cheerless chill of the morning light,
　　Out on the track where the night shades still lurk,
Ere the first gleam of the sungod's returning light
　　Round come the racehorses early at work.

Reefing and pulling and racing so readily,
　　Close sit the jockey-boys holding them hard,
"Steady the stallion there—canter him steadily,
　　Don't let him gallop so much as a yard."

Fiercely he fights while the others run wide of him,
　　Reefs at the bit that would hold him in thrall,
Plunges and bucks till the boy that's astride of him
　　Goes to the ground with a terrible fall.

"Stop him there! Block him there! Drive him in carefully,
　　Lead him about till he's quiet and cool.
Sound as a bell! though he's blown himself fearfully,
　　Now let us pick up this poor little fool.

"Stunned? Oh, by Jove, I'm afraid it's a case with him;
　　Ride for the doctor! keep bathing his head!
Send for a cart to go down to our place with him"—
　　No use! One long sigh and the little chap's dead.

Only a jockey-boy, foul-mouthed and bad you see,
　　Ignorant, heathenish, gone to his rest.
Parson or Presbyter, Pharisee, Sadducee,
　　What did you do for him?—bad was the best.

Negroes and foreigners, all have a claim on you;
　　Yearly you send your well-advertised hoard,
But the poor jockey-boy—shame on you, shame on you,
　　"Feed ye My little ones"—what said the Lord?

Him ye held less than the outer barbarian,
   Left him to die in his ignorant sin;
Have you no principles, humanitarian?
   Have you no precept—"Go gather them in?"

Knew he God's name? In his brutal profanity
   That name was an oath—out of many but one.
What did he get from our famed Christianity?
   Where has his soul—if he had any—gone?

Fourteen years old, and what was he taught of it?
   What did he know of God's infinite Grace?
Draw the dark curtain of shame o'er the thought of it
   Draw the shroud over the jockey-boy's face.

HOW M'GINNIS
WENT MISSING

LET us cease our idle chatter,
  Let the tears bedew our cheek,
For a man from Tallangatta
  Has been missing for a week.

Where the roaring flooded Murray
  Covered all the lower land,
There he started in a hurry,
  With a bottle in his hand.

And his fate is hid for ever,
  But the public seem to think
That he slumbered by the river,
  'Neath the influence of drink.

And they scarcely seem to wonder
  That the river, wide and deep,
Never woke him with its thunder,
  Never stirred him in his sleep.

As the crashing logs came sweeping
  And their tumult filled the air,
Then M'Ginnis murmured, sleeping,
  "'Tis a wake in ould Kildare."

So the river rose and found him
  Sleeping softly by the stream.
And the cruel waters drowned him
  Ere he wakened from his dream.

And the blossom-tufted wattle,
  Blooming brightly on the lea,
Saw M'Ginnis and the bottle
  Going drifting out to sea.

A VOICE FROM
THE TOWN

*A sequel to Mowbray Morris's "A Voice
from the Bush".*

I THOUGHT, in the days of my droving,
  Of steps I might hope to retrace,
To be done with the bush and the roving
  And settle once more in my place.
With a heart that was wellnigh to breaking,
  In the long, lonely rides on the plain,
I thought of the pleasure of taking
  The hand of a lady again.

I am back into civilization,
  Once more in the stir and the strife,
But the old joys have lost their sensation—
  The light has gone out of my life;
The men of my time they have married,
  Made fortunes or gone to the wall;
Too long from the scene I have tarried,
  And, somehow, I'm out of it all.

For I go to the balls and the races
  A lonely, companionless elf,
And the ladies bestow all their graces
  On others less grey than myself;
While the talk goes around I'm a dumb one
  'Midst youngsters that chatter and prate,
And they call me "The Man who was Some One
  'Way back in the year Sixty-eight".

And I look, sour and old, at the dancers
  That swing to the strains of the band,
And the ladies all give me the Lancers,
  No waltzes—I quite understand.
For matrons, intent upon matching
  Their daughters with infinite push,
Would scarce think him worthy the catching,
  The broken-down man from the bush.

New partners have come and new faces,
  And I, of the bygone brigade,
Sharply feel that oblivion my place is—
  I must lie with the rest in the shade.
And the youngsters, fresh-featured and pleasant,
  They live as we lived—fairly fast;
But I doubt if the men of the present
  Are as good as the men of the past.

Of excitement and praise they are chary,
  There is nothing much good upon earth;
Their watchword is *nil admirari*,
  They are bored from the days of their birth.
Where the life that we led was a revel
  They "wince and relent and refrain"—
I could show them the road—to the Devil,
  Were I only a youngster again.

I could show them the road where the stumps are,
  The pleasures that end in remorse,
And the game where the Devil's three trumps are
  The woman, the card, and the horse.
Shall the blind lead the blind—shall the sower
  Of wind reap the storm as of yore?
Though they get to their goal somewhat slower,
  They march where we hurried before.

For the world never learns—just as we did
  They gallantly go to their fate,
Unheeded all warnings, unheeded
  The maxims of elders sedate.
As the husbandman, patiently toiling,
  Draws a harvest each year from the soil,
So the fools grow afresh for the spoiling,
  And a new crop of thieves for the spoil.

But a truce to this dull moralizing,
  Let them drink while the drops are of gold.
I have tasted the dregs—'twere surprising
  Were the new wine to me like the old;
And I weary for lack of employment
  In idleness day after day,
For the key to the door of enjoyment
  Is Youth—and I've thrown it away.

A BUNCH
OF ROSES

ROSES ruddy and roses white,
   What are the joys that my heart discloses?
Sitting alone in the fading light
Memories come to me here tonight
   With the wonderful scent of the big red roses.

Memories come as the daylight fades
   Down on the hearth where the firelight dozes;
Flicker and flutter the lights and shades,
And I see the face of a queen of maids
   Whose memory comes with the scent of roses.

Visions arise of a scene of mirth,
   And a ball-room belle who superbly poses—
A queenly woman of queenly worth,
And I am the happiest man on earth
   With a single flower from a bunch of roses.

Only her memory lives tonight—
   God in His wisdom her young life closes;
Over her grave may the turf be light,
Cover her coffin with roses white—
   She was always fond of the big white roses.

    .   .   .   .   .

Such are the visions that fade away—
   Man proposes and God disposes;
Look in the glass and I see today
Only an old man, worn and grey,
   Bending his head to a bunch of roses.

BLACK
SWANS

As I lie at rest on a patch of clover
In the Western Park when the day is done,
I watch as the wild black swans fly over
With their phalanx turned to the sinking sun;
And I hear the clang of their leader crying
To a lagging mate in the rearward flying,
And they fade away in the darkness dying,
Where the stars are mustering one by one.

O ye wild black swans, 'twere a world of wonder
For a while to join in your westward flight,
With the stars above and the dim earth under,
Through the cooling air of the glorious night.
As we swept along on our pinions winging,
We should catch the chime of a church-bell ringing,
Or the distant note of a torrent singing,
Or the far-off flash of a station light.

From the northern lakes with the reeds and rushes,
Where the hills are clothed with a purple haze,
Where the bell-birds chime and the songs of thrushes
Make music sweet in the jungle maze,
They will hold their course to the westward ever,
Till they reach the banks of the old grey river,
Where the waters wash, and the reed-beds quiver
In the burning heat of the summer days.

O ye strange wild birds, will ye bear a greeting
To the folk that live in that western land?
Then for every sweep of your pinions beating
Ye shall bear a wish to the sunburnt band.
To the stalwart men who are stoutly fighting
With the heat and drought and the dust-storm smiting,
Yet whose life somehow has a strange inviting,
When once to the work they have put their hand.

Facing it yet! O my friend stout-hearted,
What does it matter for rain or shine,
For the hopes deferred and the gain departed?
Nothing could conquer that heart of thine.
And thy health and strength are beyond confessing
As the only joys that are worth possessing.
May the days to come be as rich in blessing
As the days we spent in the auld lang syne.

I would fain go back to the old grey river,
To the old bush days when our hearts were light;
But, alas! those days they have fled for ever,
They are like the swans that have swept from sight.
And I know full well that the strangers' faces
Would meet us now in our dearest places;
For our day is dead and has left no traces
But the thoughts that live in my mind tonight.

There are folk long dead, and our hearts would sicken—
We should grieve for them with a bitter pain;
If the past could live and the dead could quicken,
We then might turn to that life again.
But on lonely nights we should hear them calling,
We should hear their steps on the pathways falling,
We should loathe the life with a hate appalling
In our lonely rides by the ridge and plain.

    .   .   .   .   .   .

In the silent park is a scent of clover,
And the distant roar of the town is dead.
And I hear once more, as the swans fly over,
Their far-off clamour from overhead.
They are flying west, by their instinct guided,
And for man likewise is his fate decided,
And griefs apportioned and joys divided
By a mighty power with a purpose dread.

THE
ALL RIGHT UN

HE came from "further out",
That land of heat and drought
And dust and gravel.
He got a touch of sun,
And rested at the run
Until his cure was done,
And he could travel.

When spring had decked the plain,
He flitted off again
As flit the swallows.
And from that western land,
When many months were spanned,
A letter came to hand,
Which read as follows:

"Dear Sir, I take my pen
In hopes that all your men
And you are hearty.
You think that I've forgot
Your kindness, Mr Scott;
Oh, no, dear sir, I'm not
That sort of party.

"You sometimes bet, I know.
Well, now you'll have a show
The 'books' to frighten.
Up here at Wingadee
Young Billy Fife and me
We're training Strife, and he
Is a all right un.

"Just now we're running byes,
But, sir, first time he tries
I'll send you word of.
And running 'on the crook'
Their measures we have took;
It is the deadest hook
You ever heard of.

"So when we lets him go,
Why then I'll let you know,
And you can have a show
To put a mite on.
Now, sir, my leave I'll take,
Yours truly, William Blake.
P.S.—Make no mistake,
He's a all right un."

.   .   .   .

By next week's *Riverine*
I saw my friend had been
A bit too cunning.
I read: "The racehorse Strife
And jockey William Fife
Disqualified for life—
Suspicious running."

But though they spoilt his game,
I reckon all the same
I fairly ought to claim
My friend a white un.
For though he wasn't straight,
His deeds would indicate
His heart at any rate
Was "a all right un".

THE BOSS OF
THE *ADMIRAL LYNCH*

DID you ever hear tell of Chili? I was readin' the other day
Of President Balmaceda and of how he was sent away.
It seems that he didn't suit 'em—they thought that they'd like a
    change,
So they started an insurrection and chased him across the range.
They seem to be restless people—and, judging by what you hear,
They raise up these revolutions 'bout two or three times a year;
And the man that goes out of office, he goes for the boundary quick,
For there isn't no vote by ballot—it's bullets that does the trick.
And it ain't like a real battle, where the prisoners' lives are spared,
And they fight till there's one side beaten and then there's a truce
    declared,
And the man that has got the licking goes down like a blooming lord
To hand in his resignation and give up his blooming sword,
And the other man bows and takes it, and everything's all polite—
This wasn't that sort of a picnic, this wasn't that sort of a fight.
For the pris'ners they took—they shot 'em, no odds were they small
    or great;
If they'd collared old Balmaceda, they reckoned to shoot him
    straight.
A lot of bloodthirsty devils they were—but there ain't a doubt
They must have been real plucked uns, the way that they fought
    it out,
And the king of 'em all, I reckon, the man that could stand a pinch.
Was the boss of a one-horse gunboat. They called her the *Admiral
    Lynch.*

Well, he was for Balmaceda, and after the war was done,
And Balmaceda was beaten and his troops had been forced to run,
The other man fetched his army and proceeded to do things brown.
He marched 'em into the fortress and took command of the town,
Cannon and guns and horses troopin' along the road,
Rumblin' over the bridges; and never a foeman showed
Till they came in sight of the harbour—and the very first thing
    they see
Was this mite of a one-horse gunboat a-lying against the quay;
And there as they watched they noticed a flutter of crimson rag
And under their eyes he hoisted old Balmaceda's flag.

Well, I tell you it fairly knocked 'em—it just took away their
    breath,
For he must ha' known, if they caught him, 'twas nothin' but
    sudden death.
An' he'd got no fire in his furnace, no chance to put out to sea,
So he stood by his gun and waited with his vessel against the quay.
Well, they sent him a civil message to say that the war was done,
And most of his side were corpses, and all that were left had run,
And blood had been spilt sufficient; so they gave him a chance to
    decide
If he'd haul down his bit of bunting and come on the winning side.
He listened and heard their message, and answered them all polite
That he was a Spanish hidalgo, and the men of his race *must* fight!
A gunboat against an army, and with never a chance to run,
And them with their hundred cannon and him with a single gun:
The odds were a trifle heavy—but he wasn't the sort to flinch.
So he opened fire on the army, did the boss of the *Admiral Lynch*.

They pounded his boat to pieces, they silenced his single gun,
And captured the whole consignment, for none of 'em cared to run;
And it don't say whether they shot him—it don't even give his
    name—
But whatever they did I'll wager that he went to his graveyard
    game.
I tell you those old hidalgos, so stately and so polite,
They turn out the real Maginnis when it comes to an uphill fight.
There was General Alcantara, who died in the heaviest brunt,
And General Alzereca was killed in the battle's front;
But the king of 'em all, I reckon—the man that could stand a
    pinch—
Was the man who attacked the army with the gunboat *Admiral
    Lynch*.

A BUSHMAN'S SONG

I'M travelling down the Castlereagh, and I'm a station-hand,
I'm handy with the ropin' pole, I'm handy with the brand,
And I can ride a rowdy colt, or swing the axe all day,
But there's no demand for a station-hand along the Castlereagh.

So it's shift, boys, shift, for there isn't the slightest doubt
That we've got to make a shift to the stations further out,
With the pack-horse runnin' after, for he follows like a dog,
We must strike across the country at the old jig-jog.

This old black horse I'm riding—if you'll notice what's his brand,
He wears the crooked R, you see—none better in the land.
He takes a lot of beatin', and the other day we tried,
For a bit of a joke, with a racing bloke, for twenty pound a side.

It was shift, boys, shift, for there wasn't the slightest doubt
That I had to make him shift, for the money was nearly out,
But he cantered home a winner, with the other one at the flog—
He's a red-hot sort to pick up with his old jig-jog.

I asked a cove for shearin' once along the Marthaguy:
"We shear non-union here," says he. "I call it scab," says I.
I looked along the shearin' floor before I turned to go—
There were eight or ten dashed Chinamen a-shearin' in a row.

It was shift, boys, shift, for there wasn't the slightest doubt
It was time to make a shift with the leprosy about.
So I saddled up my horses, and I whistled to my dog,
And I left his scabby station at the old jig-jog.

I went to Illawarra, where my brother's got a farm;
He has to ask his landlord's leave before he lifts his arm:
The landlord owns the country-side—man, woman, dog, and cat,
They haven't the cheek to dare to speak without they touch their
    hat.

It was shift, boys, shift, for there wasn't the slightest doubt
Their little landlord god and I would soon have fallen out,
Was I to touch my hat to him?—was I his bloomin' dog?
So I makes for up the country at the old jig-jog.

But it's time that I was movin', I've a mighty way to go
Till I drink artesian water from a thousand feet below;
Till I meet the overlanders with the cattle comin' down—
And I'll work a while till I make a pile, then have a spree in town.

So it's shift, boys, shift, for there isn't the slightest doubt
We've got to make a shift to the stations further out:
The pack-horse runs behind us, for he follows like a dog,
And we cross a lot of country at the old jig-jog.

HOW
GILBERT DIED

THERE's never a stone at the sleeper's head,
  There's never a fence beside,
And the wandering stock on the grave may tread
  Unnoticed and undenied;
But the smallest child on the Watershed
  Can tell you how Gilbert died.

For he rode at dusk with his comrade Dunn
  To the hut at the Stockman's Ford;
In the waning light of the sinking sun
  They peered with a fierce accord.
They were outlaws both—and on each man's head
  Was a thousand pounds reward.

They had taken toll of the country round,
  And the troopers came behind
With a black who tracked like a human hound
  In the scrub and the ranges blind:
He could run the trail where a white man's eye
  No sign of track could find.

He had hunted them out of the One Tree Hill
  And over the Old Man Plain,
But they wheeled their tracks with a wild beast's skill,
  And they made for the range again;
Then away to the hut where their grandsire dwelt
  They rode with a loosened rein.

And their grandsire gave them a greeting bold:
  "Come in and rest in peace,
No safer place does the country hold—
  With the night pursuit must cease,
And we'll drink success to the roving boys,
  And to hell with the black police."

But they went to death when they entered there
  In the hut at the Stockman's Ford,
For their grandsire's words were as false as fair—
  They were doomed to the hangman's cord.
He had sold them both to the black police
  For the sake of the big reward.

In the depth of night there are forms that glide
   As stealthily as serpents creep,
And around the hut where the outlaws hide
   They plant in the shadows deep,
And they wait till the first faint flush of dawn
   Shall waken their prey from sleep.

But Gilbert wakes while the night is dark—
   A restless sleeper aye.
He has heard the sound of a sheep-dog's bark,
   And his horse's warning neigh,
And he says to his mate, "There are hawks abroad,
   And it's time that we went away."

Their rifles stood at the stretcher head,
   Their bridles lay to hand;
They wakened the old man out of his bed,
   When they heard the sharp command:
"In the name of the Queen lay down your arms,
   Now, Dunn and Gilbert, stand!"

Then Gilbert reached for his rifle true
   That close at hand he kept;
He pointed straight at the voice, and drew,
   But never a flash outleapt,
For the water ran from the rifle breech—
   It was drenched while the outlaws slept.

Then he dropped the piece with a bitter oath,
   And he turned to his comrade Dunn:
"We are sold," he said, "we are dead men both!—
   Still, there may be a chance for one;
I'll stop and I'll fight with the pistol here,
   You take to your heels and run."

So Dunn crept out on his hands and knees
   In the dim, half-dawning light,
And he made his way to a patch of trees,
   And was lost in the black of night;
And the trackers hunted his tracks all day,
   But they never could trace his flight.

But Gilbert walked from the open door
  In a confident style and rash;
He heard at his side the rifles roar,
  And he heard the bullets crash.
But he laughed as he lifted his pistol-hand,
  And he fired at the rifle flash.

Then out of the shadows the troopers aimed
  At his voice and the pistol sound.
With rifle flashes the darkness flamed—
  He staggered and spun around,
And they riddled his body with rifle balls
  As it lay on the blood-soaked ground.

There's never a stone at the sleeper's head,
  There's never a fence beside,
And the wandering stock on the grave may tread
  Unnoticed and undenied;
But the smallest child on the Watershed
  Can tell you how Gilbert died.

THE
FLYING GANG

I SERVED my time, in the days gone by,
   In the railway's clash and clang,
And I worked my way to the end, and I
   Was the head of the "Flying Gang".
'Twas a chosen band that was kept at hand
   In case of an urgent need;
Was it south or north, we were started forth
   And away at our utmost speed.
If word reached town that a bridge was down,
   The imperious summons rang—
"Come out with the pilot engine sharp,
   And away with the flying gang."

Then a piercing scream and a rush of steam
   As the engine moved ahead;
With measured beat by the slum and street
   Of the busy town we fled,
By the uplands bright and the homesteads white,
   With the rush of the western gale—
And the pilot swayed with the pace we made
   As she rocked on the ringing rail.
And the country children clapped their hands
   As the engine's echoes rang,
But their elders said: "There is work ahead
   When they send for the flying gang."

Then across the miles of the saltbush plain
   That gleamed with the morning dew,
Where the grasses waved like the ripening grain
   The pilot engine flew—
A fiery rush in the open bush
   Where the grade marks seemed to fly,
And the order sped on the wires ahead,
   The pilot *must* go by.
The Governor's special must stand aside,
   And the fast express go hang;
Let your orders be that the line is free
   For the boys of the flying gang.

SHEARING
AT CASTLEREAGH

THE bell is set a-ringing, and the engine gives a toot,
There's five-and-thirty shearers here a-shearing for the loot,
So stir yourselves, you penners-up, and shove the sheep along—
The musterers are fetching them a hundred thousand strong—
And make your collie dogs speak up; what would the buyers say
In London if the wool was late this year from Castlereagh?

The man that "rung" the Tubbo shed is not the ringer here,
That stripling from the Cooma-side can teach him how to shear.
They trim away the ragged locks, and rip the cutter goes,
And leaves a track of snowy fleece from brisket to the nose;
It's lovely how they peel it off with never stop nor stay,
They're racing for the ringer's place this year at Castlereagh.

The man that keeps the cutters sharp is growling in his cage,
He's always in a hurry; and he's always in a rage—
"You clumsy-fisted mutton-heads, you'd turn a fellow sick,
You pass yourselves as shearers, you were born to swing a pick.
Another broken cutter here, that's two you've broke today,
It's lovely how they peel it off with never stop nor stay,

The youngsters picking up the fleece enjoy the merry din,
They throw the classer up the fleece, he throws it to the bin;
The pressers standing by the rack are waiting for the wool,
There's room for just a couple more, the press is nearly full;
Now jump upon the lever, lads, and heave and heave away,
Another bale of golden fleece is branded "Castlereagh".

THE
WIND'S MESSAGE

THERE came a whisper down the Bland between the dawn and
    dark,
Above the tossing of the pines, above the river's flow;
It stirred the boughs of giant gums and stalwart ironbark;
It drifted where the wild ducks played amid the swamps below;
It brought a breath of mountain air from off the hills of pine,
A scent of eucalyptus trees in honey-laden bloom;
And drifting, drifting far away along the southern line
It caught from leaf and grass and fern a subtle strange perfume.

It reached the toiling city folk, but few there were that heard—
The rattle of their busy life had choked the whisper down;
And some but caught a fresh-blown breeze with scent of pine that
    stirred
A thought of blue hills far away beyond the smoky town;
And others heard the whisper pass, but could not understand
The magic of the breeze's breath that set their hearts aglow,
Nor how the roving wind could bring across the Overland
A sound of voices silent now and songs of long ago.

But some that heard the whisper clear were filled with vague unrest;
The breeze had brought its message home, they could not fixed
    abide;
Their fancies wandered all the day towards the blue hills' breast,
Towards the sunny slopes that lie along the riverside.
The mighty rolling western plains are very fair to see,
Where waving to the passing breeze the silver myalls stand,
But fairer are the giant hills, all rugged though they be,
From which the two great rivers rise that run along the Bland.

Oh, rocky range, and rugged spur, and river running clear
That swings around the sudden bends with swirl of snow-white
    foam,
Though we, your sons, are far away, we sometimes seem to hear
The message that the breezes bring to call the wanderers home.
The mountain peaks are white with snow that feeds a thousand
    rills,
Along the river-banks the maize grows tall on virgin land,
And we shall live to see once more those sunny southern hills,
And strike once more the bridle-track that leads along the Bland.

JOHNSON'S ANTIDOTE

Down along the Snakebite River where the overlanders camp,
Where the serpents are in millions, all of the most deadly stamp;
Where the station-cook in terror, nearly every time he bakes,
Mixes up among the doughboys half a dozen poison-snakes;
Where the wily free-selector walks in armour-plated pants,
And defies the stings of scorpions, and the bites of bull-dog ants:
Where the adder and the viper tear each other by the throat—
There it was that William Johnson sought his snake-bite antidote.

Johnson was a free-selector, and his brain went rather queer,
For the constant sight of serpents filled him with a deadly fear;
So he tramped his free-selection, morning, afternoon, and night,
Seeking for some great specific that would cure the serpent's bite
Till King Billy, of the Mooki, chieftain of the flour-bag head,
Told him, "Spos'n snake bite pfeller, pfeller mostly drop down dead;
Spos'n snake bite old goanna, then you watch a while you see
Old goanna cure himself with eating little pfeller tree."
"That's the cure," said William Johnson, "point me out this plant
        sublime,"
But King Billy, feeling lazy, said he'd go another time.
Thus it came to pass that Johnson, having got the tale by rote,
Followed every stray goanna seeking for the antidote.

   .   .   .   .

Loafing once beside the river, while he thought his heart would
        break,
There he saw a big goanna fight with a tiger-snake.
In and out they rolled and wriggled, bit each other, heart and
        soul,
Till the valiant old goanna swallowed his opponent whole.
Breathless, Johnson sat and watched him, saw him struggle up the
        bank,
Saw him nibbling at the branches of some bushes, green and rank;
Saw him, happy and contented, lick his lips, as off he crept,
While the bulging of his stomach showed where his opponent slept
Then a cheer of exultation burst aloud from Johnson's throat;
"Luck at last," said he, "I've struck it! 'tis the famous antidote.

"Here it is, the Grand Elixir, greatest blessing ever known—
Twenty thousand men in India die each year of snakes alone;
Think of all the foreign nations, negro, chow, and blackamoor,
Saved from sudden expiration by my wondrous snakebite cure.
It will bring me fame and fortune! In the happy days to be
Men of every clime and nation will be round to gaze on me—
Scientific men in thousands, men of mark and men of note,
Rushing down the Mooki River, after Johnson's antidote.
It will cure *delirium tremens* when the patient's eyeballs stare
At imaginary spiders, snakes which really are not there.
When he thinks he sees them wriggle, when he thinks he sees
        them bloat,
It will cure him just to think of Johnson's Snakebite Antidote."

Then he rushed to the museum, found a scientific man—
"Trot me out a deadly serpent, just the deadliest you can;
I intend to let him bite me, all the risk I will endure.
Just to prove the sterling value of my wondrous snakebite cure.
Even though an adder bit me, back to life again I'd float;
Snakes are out of date, I tell you, since I've found the antidote."
Said the scientific person, "If you really want to die,
Go ahead—but, if you're doubtful, let your sheep-dog have a try.
Get a pair of dogs and try it, let the snake give both a nip;
Give your dog the snakebite mixture, let the other fellow rip;
If he dies and yours survives him then it proves the thing is good.
Will you fetch your dog and try it?" Johnson rather thought he
        would.
So he went and fetched his canine, hauled him forward by the
        throat.
"Stump, old man," says he, "we'll show them we've the genwine
        antidote."

Both the dogs were duly loaded with the poison-gland's contents;
Johnson gave his dog the mixture, then sat down to wait events.
"Mark," he said, "in twenty minutes Stump'll be a-rushing round,
While the other wretched creature lies a corpse upon the ground."
But, alas for William Johnson! ere they'd watched a half-hour's spell
Stumpy was as dead as mutton, t'other dog was live and well.
And the scientific person hurried off with utmost speed,
Tested Johnson's drug and found it was a deadly poison-weed;
Half a tumbler killed an emu, half a spoonful killed a goat—
All the snakes on earth were harmless to that awful antidote.

Down along the Mooki River, on the overlanders' camp,
Where the serpents are in millions, all of the most deadly stamp,
Wanders, daily, William Johnson, down among those poisonous
        hordes,
Shooting every stray goanna calls them "black and yaller frauds".
And King Billy, of the Mooki, cadging for the cast-off coat,
Somehow seems to dodge the subject of the snakebite antidote.

AMBITION
AND ART

Ambition

I AM the maid of the lustrous eyes
　Of great fruition,
Whom the sons of men that are over-wise
　Have called Ambition.

And the world's success is the only goal
　I have within me;
The meanest man with the smallest soul
　May woo and win me.

For the lust of power and the pride of place
　To all I proffer.
Wilt thou take thy part in the crowded race
　For what I offer?

The choice is thine, and the world is wide—
　Thy path is lonely.
I may not lead and I may not guide—
　I urge thee only.

I am just a whip and a spur that smites
　To fierce endeavour.
In the restless days and the sleepless nights
　I urge thee ever.

Thou shalt wake from sleep with a startled cry,
　In fright unleaping
At a rival's step as it passes by
　Whilst thou art sleeping.

Honour and truth shall be overthrown
　In fierce desire;
Thou shalt use thy friend as a stepping-stone
　To mount thee higher.

When the curtain falls on the sordid strife
　That seemed so splendid,
Thou shalt look with pain on the wasted life
　That thou hast ended.

Thou hast sold thy life for a guerdon small
  In fitful flashes;
There has been reward—but the end of all
  Is dust and ashes.

For the night has come and it brings to naught
  Thy projects cherished,
And thine epitaph shall in brass be wrought—
  "He lived, and perished."

Art

I wait for thee at the outer gate,
  My love, mine only;
Wherefore tarriest thou so late
  While I am lonely?

Thou shalt seek my side with a footstep swift;
  In thee implanted
Is the love of Art and the greatest gift
  That God has granted.

And the world's concerns with its rights and
        wrongs
  Shall seem but small things—
Poet or painter, or singer of songs,
  Thine art is all things.

For the wine of life is a woman's love
  To keep beside thee;
But the love of Art is a thing above—
  A star to guide thee.

As the years go by with the love of Art
  All undiminished,
Thou shalt end thy days with a quiet heart—
  Thy work is finished.

So the painter fashions a picture strong
  That fadeth never,
And the singer singeth a wondrous song
  That lives for ever.

IN DEFENCE OF
THE BUSH

So you're back from up the country, Mister Lawson, where you
        went,
And you're cursing all the business in a bitter discontent;
Well, we grieve to disappoint you, and it makes us sad to hear
That it wasn't cool and shady—and there wasn't whips of beer,
And the looney bullock snorted when you first came into view—
Well, you know it's not so often that he sees a swell like you;
And the roads were hot and dusty, and the plains were burnt
        and brown,
And no doubt you're better suited drinking lemon-squash in town.
Yet, perchance, if you should journey down the very track you
        went
In a month or two at furthest, you would wonder what it meant;
Where the sunbaked earth was gasping like a creature in its pain
You would find the grasses waving like a field of summer grain,
And the miles of thirsty gutters, blocked with sand and choked
        with mud,
You would find them mighty rivers with a turbid, sweeping flood.
For the rain and drought and sunshine make no changes in the
        street,
In the sullen line of buildings and the ceaseless tramp of feet;
But the bush has moods and changes, as the seasons rise and fall,
And the men who know the bush-land—they are loyal through it all.

   .   .   .   .

But you found the bush was dismal and a land of no delight—
Did you chance to hear a chorus in the shearers' huts at night?
Did they "rise up William Riley" by the camp-fire's cheery blaze?
Did they rise him as we rose him in the good old droving days?
And the women of the homesteads and the men you chanced to
        meet—
Were their faces sour and saddened like the "faces in the street"?
And the "shy selector children"—were they better now or worse
Than the little city urchins who would greet you with a curse?
Is not such a life much better than the squalid street and square
Where the fallen women flaunt it in the fierce electric glare,
Where the sempstress plies her needle till her eyes are sore and red
In a filthy, dirty attic toiling on for daily bread?

Did you hear no sweeter voices in the music of the bush
Than the roar of trams and buses, and the war-whoop of "the push"?
Did the magpies rouse your slumbers with their carol sweet and
        strange?
Did you hear the silver chiming of the bell-birds on the range?
But, perchance, the wild birds' music by your senses was despised,
For you say you'll stay in townships till the bush is civilized.
Would you make it a tea-garden, and on Sundays have a band
Where the "blokes" might take their "donahs", with a "public"
        close at hand?
You had better stick to Sydney and make merry with the "push",
For the bush will never suit you, and you'll never suit the bush.

LAST WEEK

Oh, the new-chum went to the backblock run,
But he should have gone there last week.
He tramped ten miles with a loaded gun,
But of turkey or duck saw never a one,
For he should have been there last week,
  They said,
There were flocks of 'em there last week.

He wended his way to a waterfall,
And he should have gone there last week.
He carried a camera, legs and all,
But the day was hot and the stream was small,
For he should have gone there last week,
  They said,
They drowned a man there last week.

He went for a drive, and he made a start,
Which should have been made last week,
For the old horse died of a broken heart;
So he footed it home and he dragged the cart—
But the horse was all right last week,
  They said,
He trotted a match last week.

So he asked the bushies who came from afar
To visit the town last week
If they'd dine with him, and they said "Hurrah!"
But there wasn't a drop in the whisky jar—
You should have been here last week,
  He said,
I drank it all up last week!

THOSE NAMES

The shearers sat in the firelight, hearty and hale and strong,
After the hard day's shearing, passing the joke along:
The "ringer" that shore a hundred, as they never were shorn before,
And the novice who, toiling bravely, had tommy-hawked half
    a score,
The tarboy, the cook and the slushy, the sweeper that swept the
    board,
The picker-up, and the penner, with the rest of the shearing horde.
There were men from the inland stations where the skies like
    a furnace glow,
And men from the Snowy River, the land of the frozen snow;
There were swarthy Queensland drovers who reckoned all land
    by miles,
And farmers' sons from the Murray, where many a vineyard smiles.
They started at telling stories when they wearied of cards and
    games,
And to give these stories flavour they threw in some local names,
Then a man from the bleak Monaro, away on the tableland,
He fixed his eyes on the ceiling, and he started to play his hand.
He told them of Adjintoothbong, where the pine-clad mountains
    freeze,
And the weight of the snow in summer breaks branches off the
    trees,
And, as he warmed to the business, he let them have it strong—
Nimitybelle, Conargo, Wheeo, Bongongolong;
He lingered over them fondly, because they recalled to mind
A thought of the old bush homestead, and the girl that he left
    behind.
Then the shearers all sat silent till a man in the corner rose;
Said he "I've travelled a-plenty but never heard names like those.
Out in the western districts, out on the Castlereagh
Most of the names are easy—short for a man to say.
You've heard of Mungrybambone and the Gundabluey pine,
Quobbotha, Girilambone, and Terrramungamine,
Quambone, Eunonyhareenyha, Wee Waa, and Buntijo—"
But the rest of the shearers stopped him: "For the sake of your
    jaw, go slow,

If you reckon those names are short ones out where such names
      prevail,
Just try and remember some long ones before you begin the tale."
And the man from the western district, though never a word he
      said,
Just winked with his dexter eyelid, and then he retired to bed.

A BUSH CHRISTENING

On the outer Barcoo where the churches are few,
  And men of religion are scanty,
On a road never cross'd 'cept by folk that are lost
  One Michael Magee had a shanty.

Now this Mike was the dad of a ten-year-old lad,
  Plump, healthy, and stoutly conditioned;
He was strong as the best, but poor Mike had no rest
  For the youngster had never been christened.

And his wife used to cry, "If the darlin' should die
  Saint Peter would not recognize him."
But by luck he survived till a preacher arrived,
  Who agreed straightaway to baptize him.

Now the artful young rogue, while they held their collogue,
  With his ear to the keyhole was listenin';
And he muttered in fright, while his features turned white,
  "What the divil and all is this christenin'?"

He was none of your dolts—he had seen them brand colts.
  And it seemed to his small understanding,
If the man in the frock made him one of the flock,
  It must mean something very like branding.

So away with a rush he set off for the bush,
  While the tears in his eyelids they glistened—
"'Tis outrageous," says he, "to brand youngsters like me;
  I'll be dashed if I'll stop to be christened!"

Like a young native dog he ran into a log,
  And his father with language uncivil,
Never heeding the "praste", cried aloud in his haste
  "Come out and be christened, you divil!"

But he lay there as snug as a bug in a rug,
  And his parents in vain might reprove him,
Till his reverence spoke (he was fond of a joke)
  "I've a notion," says he, "that'll move him.

"Poke a stick up the log, give the spalpeen a prog;
　　Poke him aisy—don't hurt him or maim him;
'Tis not long that he'll stand, I've the water at hand,
　　As he rushes out this end I'll name him.

"Here he comes, and for shame! ye've forgotten the name—
　　Is it Patsy or Michael or Dinnis?"
Here the youngster ran out, and the priest gave a shout—
　　"Take your chance, anyhow, wid 'Maginnis!' "

As the howling young cub ran away to the scrub
　　Where he knew that pursuit would be risky,
The priest, as he fled, flung a flask at his head
　　That was labelled "Maginnis's Whisky"!

Now Maginnis Magee has been made a J.P.,
　　And the one thing he hates more than sin is
To be asked by the folk, who have heard of the joke,
　　How he came to be christened Maginnis!

HOW THE FAVOURITE BEAT US

"Ay," said the boozer, "I tell you, it's true, sir,
I once was a punter with plenty of pelf,
But gone is my glory; I'll tell you the story
How I stiffened my horse and got stiffened myself.

"'Twas a mare called The Cracker, I came down to back
        her,
But found she was favourite all of a rush;
The folk just did pour on to lay six to four on,
And several bookies were killed in the crush.

"It seems old Tomato was stiff, though a starter;
They reckoned him fit for the Caulfield to keep.
The Bloke and The Donah were scratched by their owner—
He only was offered three-fourths of the sweep.

"We knew Salamander was slow as a gander,
The mare could have beat him the length of the straight,
And old Manumission was out of condition,
And most of the others were running off weight.

"No doubt some one 'blew it', for everyone knew it;
The bets were all gone, and I muttered in spite
'If I can't get a copper, by Jingo, I'll stop her!
Let the public fall in, it will serve the brutes right.'

"I said to the jockey, 'Now listen, my cocky,
You watch as you're cantering down by the stand;
I'll wait where that toff is and give you the office,
You're only to win if I lift up my hand.'

"I then tried to back her—What price is The Cracker?
'Our books are at full, sir,' each bookie did swear;
My mind, then, I made up, my fortune I played up,
I bet every shilling against my own mare.

"I strolled to the gateway; the mare in the straightway
Was shifting and dancing, and pawing the ground;
The boy saw me enter and wheeled for his canter,
When a darned great mosquito came buzzing around.

85

"They breed 'em at Hexham, it's risky to vex 'em,
They suck a man dry at a sitting, no doubt;
But just as the mare passed, he fluttered my hair past—
I lifted my hand, and I flattened him out.

"I was stunned when they started; the mare simply darted
Away to the front when the flag was let fall,
For none there could match her, and none tried to catch
       her—
She finished a furlong in front of them all.

"You bet that I went for the boy, whom I sent for
The moment he weighed and came out of the stand—
'Who paid you to win it? Come, own up this minute.'
'Lord love yer,' said he 'why you lifted your hand.'

" 'Twas true, by St Peter; that cursed 'musketeer'
Had broke me so broke that I hadn't a brown;
And you'll find the best course is when dealing with horses
To win when you're able, and *keep your hands down*."

THE
GREAT CALAMITY

MacFierce'un came to Whiskeyhurst
  When summer days were hot,
And bided there wi' Jock MacThirst,
  A brawny brother Scot.
Good faith! They made the whisky fly
  Like Highland chieftains true,
And when they'd drunk the beaker dry
  They sang "We are nae fou!
There's nae folk like oor ain folk,
  Sae gallant and sae true."
They sang the only Scottish joke
  Which is "We are nae fou".
Said bold MacThirst, "Let Saxons jaw
  Aboot their great concerns,
But Bonnie Scotland beats them a',
  The Land o' Cakes and Burns,
The land of pairtridge, deer, and grouse;
  Fill up your glass, I beg,
There's muckle whuskey i' the house,
  Forbye what's in the keg."
And here a hearty laugh he laughed,
  "Just come wi' me, I beg."
MacFierce'un saw with pleasure daft
  A fifty-gallon keg.

"Losh, man, that's graund," MacFierce'un cried,
  "Saw ever man the like,
Noo, wi' the daylicht, I maun ride
  To meet a Southron tyke,
But I'll be back ere summer's gone,
  So bide for me, I beg;
We'll mak' a graund assault upon
  Yon deevil of a keg."

   .   .   .   .   .   .

MacFierce'un rode to Whiskeyhurst
  When summer days were gone,
And there he met with Jock MacThirst
  Was greetin' all alone.

"MacThirst, what gars ye look sae blank?
 Hae all your wuts gane daft?
Has that accursed Southron bank
 Called up your overdraft?
Is all your grass burnt up wi' drouth?
 Is wool and hides gane flat?"
MacThirst replied, "Guid friend, in truth,
 'Tis muckle waur than that."

"Has sair misfortune cursed your life
 That you should weep sae free?
Is harm upon your bonnie wife,
 The children at your knee?
Is scaith upon your house and hame?"
 MacThirst upraised his head:
"My bairns hae done the deed of shame—
 'Twere better they were dead.
To think my bonnie infant son
 Should do the deed o' guilt—
*He let the whuskey spigot run,
 And a' the whuskey's spilt!*"

   .   .   .   .   .

Upon them both these words did bring
 A solemn silence deep;
Good faith, it is a fearsome thing
 To see two strong men weep.

COME-BY-CHANCE

As I pondered very weary o'er a volume long and dreary—
For the plot was void of interest; 'twas the Postal Guide, in fact—
There I learnt the true location, distance, size, and population
Of each township, town, and village in the radius of the Act.

And I learnt that Puckawidgee stands beside the Murrumbidgee,
And the Booleroi and Bumble get their letters twice a year,
Also that the post inspector, when he visited Collector,
Closed the office up instanter, and re-opened Dungalear.

But my languid mood forsook me, when I found a name that
    took me;
Quite by chance I came across it— "Come-by-Chance" was what
    I read;
No location was assigned it, not a thing to help one find it,
Just an N which stood for northward, and the rest was all unsaid.

I shall leave my home, and forthward wander stoutly to the
    northward
Till I come by chance across it, and I'll straightway settle down;
For there can't be any hurry, nor the slightest cause for worry
Where the telegraph don't reach you nor the railways run to town.

And one's letters and exchanges come by chance across the ranges,
Where a wiry young Australian leads a pack-horse once a week,
And the good news grows by keeping, and you're spared the
    pain of weeping
Over bad news when the mailman drops the letters in the creek.

But I fear, and more's the pity, that there's really no such city,
For there's not a man can find it of the shrewdest folk I know;
"Come-by-Chance", be sure it never means a land of fierce
    endeavour—
It is just the careless country where the dreamers only go.

    .   .   .   .   .   .

Though we work and toil and hustle in our life of haste and
    bustle,
All that makes our life worth living comes unstriven for and free;
Man may weary and importune, but the fickle goddess Fortune
Deals him out his pain or pleasure, careless what his worth may be.

All the happy times entrancing, days of sport and nights of dancing,
Moonlit rides and stolen kisses, pouting lips and loving glance:
When you think of these be certain you have looked behind the
    curtain,
You have had the luck to linger just a while in "Come-by-Chance".

UNDER THE SHADOW OF KILEY'S HILL

THIS is the place where they all were bred;
  Some of the rafters are standing still;
Now they are scattered and lost and dead,
Every one from the old nest fled,
  Out of the shadow of Kiley's Hill.

Better it is that they ne'er came back—
  Changes and chances are quickly rung;
Now the old homestead is gone to rack,
Green is the grass on the well-worn track
  Down by the gate where the roses clung.

Gone is the garden they kept with care;
  Left to decay at its own sweet will,
Fruit-trees and flower-beds eaten bare,
Cattle and sheep where the roses were,
  Under the shadow of Kiley's Hill.

Where are the children that strove and grew
  In the old homestead in days gone by?
One is away on the far Barcoo
Watching his cattle the long year through,
  Watching them starve in the droughts and die.

One, in the town where all cares are rife,
  Weary with troubles that cramp and kill,
Fain would be done with the restless strife,
Fain would go back to the old bush life,
  Back to the shadow of Kiley's Hill.

One is away on the roving quest,
  Seeking his share of the golden spoil;
Out in the wastes of the trackless west,
Wandering ever he gives the best
  Of his years and strength to the hopeless toil.

What of the parents? That unkept mound
  Shows where they slumber united still;
Rough is their grave, but they sleep as sound
Out on the range as in holy ground,
  Under the shadow of Kiley's Hill.

JIM CAREW

Born of a thoroughbred English race,
  Well proportioned and closely knit,
Neat, slim figure and handsome face,
  Always ready and always fit,
Hardy and wiry of limb and thew,
That was the ne'er-do-well Jim Carew.

One of the sons of the good old land—
  Many a year since his like was known;
Never a game but he took command,
  Never a sport but he held his own;
Gained at his college a triple blue—
Good as they make them was Jim Carew.

Came to grief—was it card or horse?
  Nobody asked and nobody cared;
Ship him away to the bush of course,
  Ne'er-do-well fellows are easily spared;
Only of women a sorrowing few
Wept at parting from Jim Carew.

Gentleman Jim on the cattle-camp,
  Sitting his horse with an easy grace;
But the reckless living has left its stamp
  In the deep drawn lines of that handsome face,
And the harder look in those eyes of blue:
Prompt at a quarrel is Jim Carew.

Billy the Lasher was out for gore—
  Twelve-stone navvy with chest of hair—
When he opened out with a hungry roar
  On a ten-stone man, it was hardly fair;
But his wife was wise if his face she knew
By the time you were done with him, Jim Carew.

Gentleman Jim in the stockmen's hut
  Works with them, toils with them, side by side;
As to his past—well, his lips are shut.
  "Gentleman once," say his mates with pride,
And the wildest Cornstalk can ne'er outdo
In feats of recklessness Jim Carew.

What should he live for? A dull despair!
   Drink is his master and drags him down,
Water of Lethe that drowns all care.
   Gentleman Jim has a lot to drown,
And he reigns as king with a drunken crew,
Sinking to misery, Jim Carew.

Such is the end of the ne'er-do-well—
   Jimmy the Boozer, all down at heel;
But he straightens up when he's asked to tell
   His name and race, and a flash of steel
Still lightens up in those eyes of blue—
"I am, or—no, I *was*—Jim Carew."

THE
SWAGMAN'S REST

We buried old Bob where the bloodwoods wave
  At the foot of the Eaglehawk;
We fashioned a cross on the old man's grave
  For fear that his ghost might walk;
We carved his name on a bloodwood tree
  With the date of his sad decease
And in place of "Died from effects of spree"
  We wrote "May he rest in peace".

For Bob was known on the Overland,
  A regular old bush wag,
Tramping along in the dust and sand,
  Humping his well-worn swag.
He would camp for days in the river-bed,
  And loiter and "fish for whales".
"I'm into the swagman's yard," he said.
  "And I never shall find the rails."

But he found the rails on that summer night
  For a better place—or worse,
As we watched by turns in the flickering light
  With an old black gin for nurse.
The breeze came in with the scent of pine,
  The river sounded clear,
When a change came on, and we saw the sign
  That told us the end was near.

He spoke in a cultured voice and low—
  "I fancy they've 'sent the route';
I once was an army man, you know.
  Though now I'm a drunken brute;
But bury me out where the bloodwoods wave,
  And, if ever you're fairly stuck,
Just take and shovel me out of the grave
  And, maybe, I'll bring you luck.

"For I've always heard—" here his voice grew weak,
    His strength was wellnigh sped,
He gasped and struggled and tried to speak,
    Then fell in a moment—dead.
Thus ended a wasted life and hard,
    Of energies misapplied—
Old Bob was out of the "swagman's yard"
    And over the Great Divide.

.   .   .   .   .

The drought came down on the field and flock,
    And never a raindrop fell,
Though the tortured moans of the starving stock
    Might soften a fiend from hell.
And we thought of the hint that the swagman gave
    When he went to the Great Unseen—
We shovelled the skeleton out of the grave
    To see what his hint might mean.

We dug where the cross and the grave posts were,
    We shovelled away the mould,
When sudden a vein of quartz lay bare
    All gleaming with yellow gold.
'Twas a reef with never a fault nor baulk
    That ran from the range's crest,
And the richest mine on the Eaglehawk
    Is known as "The Swagman's Rest".

DAYLIGHT
IS DYING

The daylight is dying
  Away in the west,
The wild birds are flying
  In silence to rest;
In leafage and frondage
  Where shadows are deep,
They pass to its bondage—
  The kingdom of sleep.

And watched in their sleeping
  By stars in the height,
They rest in your keeping,
  O wonderful night.
When night doth her glories
  Of starshine unfold,
'Tis then that the stories
  Of bush-land are told.

Unnumbered I hold them
  In memories bright,
But who could unfold them,
  Or read them aright?
Beyond all denials
  The stars in their glories,
The breeze in the myalls,
  Are part of these stories.

The waving of grasses,
  The song of the river
That sings as it passes
  For ever and ever,
The hobble-chains' rattle,
  The calling of birds,
The lowing of cattle
  Must blend with the words.

"Angel Harrison's black gelding Pardon",
from *Old Pardon the Son of Reprieve*—Norman Lindsay's first submission
for the cover of *The Man from Snowy River*

Without these, indeed, you
   Would find it ere long,
As though I should read you
   The words of a song
That lamely would linger
   When lacking the rune,
The voice of a singer,
   The lilt of the tune.

But, as one half-hearing
   An old-time refrain,
With memory clearing,
   Recalls it again,
These tales roughly wrought of
   The Bush and its ways,
May call back a thought of
   The wandering days;

And, blending with each
   In the memories that throng
There haply shall reach
   You some echo of song.

II
RIO GRANDE
AND OTHER VERSES

RIO GRANDE

Now this was what Macpherson told
  While waiting in the stand;
A reckless rider, over-bold,
The only man with hands to hold
  The rushing Rio Grande.

He said, "This day I bid good-bye
  To bit and bridle rein,
To ditches deep and fences high,
For I have dreamed a dream, and I
  Shall never ride again.

"I dreamt last night I rode this race
  That I today must ride,
And cantering down to take my place
I saw full many an old friend's face
  Come stealing to my side.

"Dead men on horses long since dead,
  They clustered on the track;
The champions of the days long fled,
They moved around with noiseless tread—
  Bay, chestnut, brown, and black.

"And one man on a big grey steed
  Rode up and waved his hand;
Said he, 'We help a friend in need,
And we have come to give a lead
  To you and Rio Grande.

"'For you must give the field the slip;
  So never draw the rein,
But keep him moving with the whip,
And, if he falter, set your lip
  And rouse him up again.

"'But when you reach the big stone wall
  Put down your bridle-hand
And let him sail—he cannot fall,
But don't you interfere at all;
  You trust old Rio Grande.'

"We started, and in front we showed,
    The big horse running free:
Right fearlessly and game he strode,
And by my side those dead men rode
    Whom no one else could see.

"As silently as flies a bird,
    They rode on either hand;
At every fence I plainly heard
The phantom leader give the word,
    'Make room for Rio Grande!'

"I spurred him on to get the lead,
    I chanced full many a fall;
But swifter still each phantom steed
Kept with me, and at racing speed
    We reached the big stone wall.

"And there the phantoms on each side
    Drew in and blocked his leap;
'Make room! make room!' I loudly cried
But right in front they seemed to ride—
    I cursed them in my sleep.

"He never flinched, he faced it game,
    He struck it with his chest,
And every stone burst out in flame—
And Rio Grande and I became
    Phantoms among the rest.

"And then I woke, and for a space
    All nerveless did I seem;
For I have ridden many a race
But never one at such a pace
    As in that fearful dream.

"And I am sure as man can be
    That out upon the track
Those phantoms that men cannot see
Are waiting now to ride with me;
    And I shall not come back

"For I must ride the dead men's race,
    And follow their command;
'Twere worse than death, the foul disgrace
If I should fear to take my place
    Today on Rio Grande."

He mounted, and a jest he threw,
    With never sign of gloom;
But all who heard the story knew
That Jack Macpherson, brave and true,
    Was going to his doom.

They started, and the big black steed
    Came flashing past the stand;
All single-handed in the lead
He strode along at racing speed,
    The mighty Rio Grande.

But on his ribs the whalebone stung—
    A madness, sure, it seemed—
And soon it rose on every tongue
That Jack Macpherson rode among
    The creatures he had dreamed.

He looked to left, and looked to right,
    As though men rode beside;
And Rio Grande, with foam-flecks white,
Raced at his jumps in headlong flight
    And cleared them in his stride.

But when they reached the big stone wall,
    Down went the bridle-hand,
And loud we heard Macpherson call
"Make room, or half the field will fall!
    Make room for Rio Grande!"

"He's down! he's down!" And horse and man
    Lay quiet side by side!
No need the pallid face to scan,
We knew with Rio Grande he ran
    The race the dead men ride.

WITH FRENCH
TO KIMBERLEY

THE Boers were down on Kimberley with siege and Maxim gun;
The Boers were down on Kimberley, their numbers ten to one!
Faint were the hopes the British had to make the struggle good—
Defenceless in an open plain the Diamond City stood.
They built them forts with bags of sand, they fought from roof and
     wall,
They flashed a message to the south, "Help! or the town must fall!"
Then down our ranks the order ran to march at dawn of day,
And French was off to Kimberley to drive the Boers away.

He made no march along the line; he made no front attack
Upon those Magersfontein heights that held the Seaforths back;
But eastward over pathless plains, by open veldt and vley.
Across the front of Cronje's force his troopers held their way.
The springbuck, feeding on the flats where Modder River runs,
Were startled by his horses' hoofs, the rumble of his guns.
The Dutchman's spies that watched his march from every rocky
     wall
Rode back in haste: "He marches East! He threatens Jacobsdal!"
Then north he wheeled as wheels the hawk, and showed to their
     dismay
That French was off to Kimberley to drive the Boers away.

His column was five thousand strong—all mounted men—and guns:
There met, beneath the world-wide flag, the world-wide Empire's
     sons;
They came to prove to all the earth that kinship conquers space,
And those who fight the British Isles must fight the British race!
From far New Zealand's flax and fern, from cold Canadian snows,
From Queensland plains, where hot as fire the summer sunshine
     glows—
And in the front the Lancers rode that New South Wales had sent:
With easy stride across the plain their long, lean Walers went.
Unknown, untried, those squadrons were, but proudly out they drew
Beside the English regiments that fought at Waterloo.
From every coast, from every clime, they met in proud array
To go with French to Kimberley to drive the Boers away.

He crossed the Reit and fought his way towards the Modder bank.
The foemen closed behind his march, and hung upon the flank.
The long, dry grass was all ablaze (and fierce the veldt fire runs);
He fought them through a wall of flame that blazed around the
      guns!
Then limbered up and drove at speed, though horses fell and died;
We might not halt for man nor beast on that wild, daring ride.
Black with the smoke and parched with thirst, we pressed the
      livelong day
Our headlong march to Kimberley to drive the Boers away.

We reached the drift at fall of night, and camped across the ford.
Next day from all the hills around the Dutchman's cannon roared.
A narrow pass ran through the hills, with guns on either side;
The boldest man might well turn pale before that pass he tried,
For, if the first attack should fail, then every hope was gone:
But French looked once, and only once, and then he said, "Push on!"
The gunners plied their guns amain; the hail of shrapnel flew;
With rifle fire and lancer charge their squadrons back we threw;
And through the pass between the hills we swept in furious fray,
And French was through to Kimberley to drive the Boers away.

Ay, French was through to Kimberley! And ere the day was done
We saw the Diamond City stand, lit by the evening sun:
Above the town the heliograph hung like an eye of flame:
Around the town the foemen camped—they knew not that we came;
But soon they saw us, rank on rank; they heard our squadrons' tread;
In panic fear they left their tents, in hopeless rout they fled—
And French rode into Kimberley; the people cheered amain,
The women came with tear-stained eyes to touch his bridle rein,
The starving children lined the streets to raise a feeble cheer,
The bells rang out a joyous peal to say "Relief is here!"
Ay! we that saw that stirring march are proud that we can say
We went with French to Kimberley to drive the Boers away.

BY THE GREY
GULF-WATER

FAR to the Northward there lies a land,
  A wonderful land that the winds blow over,
And none may fathom or understand
  The charm it holds for the restless rover;
A great grey chaos—a land half made,
  Where endless space is and no life stirreth;
There the soul of a man will recoil afraid
  From the sphinx-like visage that Nature weareth.
But old Dame Nature, though scornful, craves
  Her dole of death and her share of slaughter;
Many indeed are the nameless graves
  Where her victims sleep by the Grey Gulf-water.

Slowly and slowly those grey streams glide,
  Drifting along with a languid motion,
Lapping the reed-beds on either side,
  Wending their way to the North Ocean.
Grey are the plains where the emus pass
  Silent and slow, with their staid demeanour;
Over the dead men's graves the grass
  Maybe is waving a trifle greener.
Down in the world where men toil and spin
  Dame Nature smiles as man's hand has taught her;
Only the dead men her smiles can win
  In the great lone land by the Grey Gulf-water.

For the strength of man is an insect's strength
  In the face of that mighty plain and river,
And the life of a man is a moment's length
  To the life of the stream that will run for ever.
And so it comes that they take no part
  In small world worries; each hardy rover
Rides like a paladin, light of heart,
  With the plains around and the blue sky over.
And up in the heavens the brown lark sings
  The songs that the strange wild land has taught her;
Full of thanksgiving her sweet song rings—
  And I wish I were back by the Grey Gulf-water.

WITH
THE CATTLE

THE drought is down on field and flock,
   The river-bed is dry;
And we must shift the starving stock
   Before the cattle die.
We muster up with weary hearts
   At breaking of the day,
And turn our heads to foreign parts,
   To take the stock away.
     And it's hunt 'em up and dog 'em,
     And it's get the whip and flog 'em,
For it's weary work, is droving, when they're
       dying every day;
     By stock routes bare and eaten,
     On dusty roads and beaten,
With half a chance to save their lives we take
       the stock away.

We cannot use the whip for shame
   On beasts that crawl along;
We have to drop the weak and lame,
   And try to save the strong;
The wrath of God is on the track,
   The drought fiend holds his sway;
With blows and cries and stockwhip crack
   We take the stock away.
     As they fall we leave them lying,
     With the crows to watch them dying,
Grim sextons of the Overland that fasten on
       their prey;
     By the fiery dust-storm drifting,
     And the mocking mirage shifting,
In heat and drought and hopeless pain we take
       the stock away.

In dull despair the days go by
　　With never hope of change,
But every stage we feel more nigh
　　The distant mountain range;
And some may live to climb the pass,
　　And reach the great plateau,
And revel in the mountain grass
　　By streamlets fed with snow.
　　　　As the mountain wind is blowing
　　　　It starts the cattle lowing
And calling to each other down the dusty long
　　　　　　array;
　　　　And there speaks a grizzled drover:
　　　　"Well, thank God, the worst is over,
The creatures smell the mountain grass that's
　　　　twenty miles away."

They press towards the mountain grass,
　　They look with eager eyes
Along the rugged stony pass
　　That slopes towards the skies;
Their feet may bleed from rocks and stones,
　　But, though the blood-drop starts,
They struggle on with stifled groans,
　　For hope is in their hearts.
　　　　And the cattle that are leading,
　　　　Though their feet are worn and bleeding,
Are breaking to a kind of run—pull up, and let
　　　　them go!
　　　　For the mountain wind is blowing,
　　　　And the mountain grass is growing,
They'll settle down by running streams ice-cold
　　　　with melted snow.

　　　　．　　　．　　　．　　　．　　　．　　　．

The days are gone of heat and drought
　　Upon the stricken plain;
The wind has shifted right about,
　　And brought the welcome rain;
The river runs with sullen roar,
　　All flecked with yellow foam,
And we must take the road once more

To bring the cattle home.
  And it's "Lads! we'll raise a chorus,
  There's a pleasant trip before us."
And the horses bound beneath us as we start
   them down the track;
  And the drovers canter, singing,
  Through the sweet green grasses springing
Towards the far-off mountain-land, to bring the
   cattle back.

Are these the beasts we brought away
 That move so lively now?
They scatter off like flying spray
 Across the mountain's brow;
And dashing down the rugged range
 We hear the stockwhips crack—
Good faith, it is a welcome change
 To bring such cattle back.
  And it's "Steady down the lead there!"
  And it's "Let 'em stop and feed there!"
For they're wild as mountain eagles, and their
   sides are all afoam;
  But they're settling down already,
  And they'll travel nice and steady;
With cheery call and jest and song we fetch
   the cattle home.

We have to watch them close at night
 For fear they'll make a rush,
And break away in headlong flight
 Across the open bush;
And by the camp-fire's cheery blaze,
 With mellow voice and strong,
We hear the lonely watchman raise
 The Overlander's song:
  "Oh! it's when we're done with roving,
  With the camping and the droving,
It's homeward down the Bland we'll go, and
   never more we'll roam";
  While the stars shine out above us,
  Like the eyes of those who love us—
The eyes of those who watch and wait to greet
   the cattle home.

The plains are all awave with grass,
    The skies are deepest blue;
And leisurely the cattle pass
    And feed the long day through;
But when we sight the station gate
    We make the stockwhips crack,
A welcome sound to those who wait
    To greet the cattle back:
        And through the twilight falling
        We hear their voices calling,
As the cattle splash across the ford and churn
            it into foam;
        And the children run to meet us,
        And our wives and sweethearts greet us,
Their heroes from the Overland who brought
            the cattle home.

THE
FIRST SURVEYOR

"The opening of the railway line!—the Governor and all!
With flags and banners down the street, a banquet and a ball.
Hark to 'em at the station now! They're raising cheer on cheer!
The man who brought the railway through—our friend the
      engineer.'

"They cheer *his* pluck and enterprise and engineering skill!
'Twas my old husband found the pass behind that big red hill.
Before the engineer was born we'd settled with our stock
Behind that great big mountain chain, a line of range and rock—
A line that kept us starving there in weary weeks of drought,
With ne'er a track across the range to let the cattle out.

" 'Twas then, with horses starved and weak and scarcely fit to crawl,
My husband went to find a way across the rocky wall.
He vanished in the wilderness—God knows where he was gone—
He hunted till his food gave out, but still he battled on.
His horses strayed ('twas well they did), they made towards the
      grass,
And down behind that big red hill they found an easy pass.

"He followed up and blazed the trees, to show the safest track,
Then drew his belt another hole and turned and started back.
His horses died—just one pulled through with nothing much to
      spare;
God bless the beast that brought him home, the old white Arab
      mare!
We drove the cattle through the hills, along the new-found way,
And this was our first camping-ground—just where I live today.

"Then others came across the range and built the township here,
And then there came the railway line and this young engineer;
He drove about with tents and traps, a cook to cook his meals,
A bath to wash himself at night, a chain-man at his heels.
And that was all the pluck and skill for which he's cheered and
      praised,
For after all he took the track, the same my husband blazed!

"My poor old husband, dead and gone with never feast nor cheer;
He's buried by the railway line!—I wonder can he hear
When by the very track he marked, and close to where he's laid,
The cattle trains go roaring down the one-in-thirty grade.
I wonder does he hear them pass, and can he see the sight
When, whistling shrill, the fast express goes flaming by at night.

"I think 'twould comfort him to know there's someone left to care;
I'll take some things this very night and hold a banquet there—
The hard old fare we've often shared together, him and me,
Some damper and a bite of beef, a pannikin of tea:
We'll do without the bands and flags, the speeches and the fuss,
We know who *ought* to get the cheers—and that's enough for us.

"What's that? They wish that I'd come down—the oldest settler here!
Present me to the Governor and that young engineer!
Well, just you tell his Excellence, and put the thing polite,
I'm sorry, but I can't come down—I'm dining out tonight!"

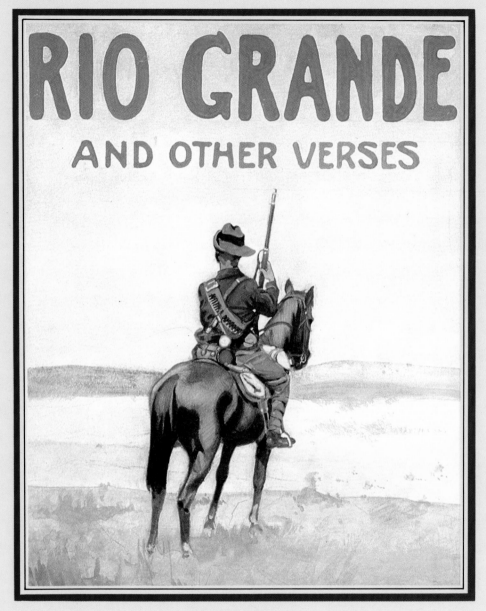

Hal Gye's jacket for
Rio Grande and other Verses

MULGA BILL'S
BICYCLE

'Twas Mulga Bill, from Eaglehawk, that caught the cycling craze;
He turned away the good old horse that served him many days;
He dressed himself in cycling clothes, resplendent to be seen;
He hurried off to town and bought a shining new machine;
And as he wheeled it through the door, with air of lordly pride,
The grinning shop assistant said, "Excuse me, can you ride?"

"See here, young man," said Mulga Bill, "from Walgett to the sea,
From Conroy's Gap to Castlereagh, there's none can ride like me.
I'm good all round at everything, as everybody knows,
Although I'm not the one to talk—I hate a man that blows.

"But riding is my special gift, my chiefest, sole delight;
Just ask a wild duck can it swim, a wild cat can it fight.
There's nothing clothed in hair or hide, or built of flesh or steel,
There's nothing walks or jumps, or runs, on axle, hoof, or wheel,
But what I'll sit, while hide will hold and girths and straps are tight;
I'll ride this here two-wheeled concern right straight away at sight."

'Twas Mulga Bill, from Eaglehawk, that sought his own abode,
That perched above the Dead Man's Creek, beside the mountain
          road.
He turned the cycle down the hill and mounted for the fray,
But ere he'd gone a dozen yards it bolted clean away.
It left the track, and through the trees, just like a silver streak,
It whistled down the awful slope towards the Dead Man's Creek.

It shaved a stump by half an inch, it dodged a big white-box:
The very wallaroos in fright went scrambling up the rocks,
The wombats hiding in their caves dug deeper underground,
But Mulga Bill, as white as chalk, sat tight to every bound.
It struck a stone and gave a spring that cleared a fallen tree,
It raced beside a precipice as close as close could be;
And then, as Mulga Bill let out one last despairing shriek,
It made a leap of twenty feet into the Dead Man's Creek.

'Twas Mulga Bill, from Eaglehawk, that slowly swam ashore:
He said, "I've had some narrer shaves and lively rides before;
I've rode a wild bull round a yard to win a five-pound bet,
But this was sure the derndest ride that I've encountered yet.
I'll give that two-wheeled outlaw best; it's shaken all my nerve
To feel it whistle through the air and plunge and buck and swerve,
It's safe at rest in Dead Man's Creek—we'll leave it lying still;
A horse's back is good enough henceforth for Mulga Bill."

THE
PEARL DIVER

KANZO MAKAME, the diver, sturdy and small Japanee,
Seeker of pearls and of pearl-shell down in the depths of the sea,
Trudged o'er the bed of the ocean, searching industriously.

Over the pearl-grounds the lugger drifted—a little white speck:
Joe Nagasaki, the "tender", holding the life-line on deck,
Talked through the rope to the diver, knew when to drift or to check.

Kanzo was king of his lugger, master and diver in one,
Diving wherever it pleased him, taking instructions from none;
Hither and thither he wandered, steering by stars and by sun.

Fearless he was beyond credence, looking at death eye to eye:
This was his formula always, "All man go dead by and by—
S'posing time come no can help it—s'pose time no come, then no
    die."

Dived in the depths of the Darnleys, down twenty fathom and five;
Down where by law, and by reason, men are forbidden to dive;
Down in a pressure so awful that only the strongest survive:

Sweated four men at the air pumps, fast as the handles could go,
Forcing the air down that reached him heated and tainted, and
    slow—
Kanzo Makame the diver stayed seven minutes below;

Came up on deck like a dead man, paralysed body and brain;
Suffered, while blood was returning, infinite tortures of pain:
Sailed once again to the Darnleys—laughed and descended again!

     .   .   .   .   .

Scarce grew the shell in the shallows, rarely a patch could they
    touch;
Always the take was so little, always the labour so much;
Always they thought of the Islands held by the lumbering Dutch—

Islands where shell was in plenty lying in passage and bay,
Islands where divers could gather hundreds of shell in a day.
But the lumbering Dutch in their gunboats they hunted the divers
    away.

Joe Nagasaki, the "tender", finding the profits grow small,
Said, "Let us go to the Islands, try for a number one haul!
If we get caught, go to prison—let them take lugger and all!"

Kanzo Makame, the diver—knowing full well what it meant—
Fatalist, gambler, and stoic, smiled a broad smile of content,
Flattened in mainsail and foresail, and off to the Islands they went.

Close to the headlands they drifted, picking up shell by the ton,
Piled up on deck were the oysters, opening wide in the sun,
When, from the lee of the headland, boomed the report of a gun.

Then if the diver was sighted, pearl-shell and lugger must go—
Joe Nagasaki decided (quick was the word and the blow),
Cut both the pipe and the life-line, leaving the diver below!

Kanzo Makame, the diver, failing to quite understand,
Pulled the "haul up" on the life-line, found it was slack in his hand;
Then, like a little brown stoic, lay down and died on the sand.

Joe Nagasaki, the "tender", smiling a sanctified smile,
Headed her straight for the gunboat—throwing out shells all the
        while—
Then went aboard and reported, "No makee dive in three mile!

"Dress no have got and no helmet—diver go shore on the spree;
Plenty wind come and break rudder—lugger get blown out to sea:
Take me to Japanee Consul, he help a poor Japanee!"

.   .   .   .   .

So the Dutch let him go; but they watched him, as off from the
        Islands he ran,
Doubting him much—but what would you? You have to be sure
        of your man
Ere you wake up that nest-ful of hornets—the little brown men of
        Japan.

Down in the ooze and the coral, down where earth's wonders are
        spread,
Helmeted, ghastly, and swollen, Kanzo Makame lies dead.
Joe Nagasaki, his "tender", is owner and diver instead.

Wearer of pearls in your necklace, comfort yourself if you can.
These are the risks of the pearling—these are the ways of Japan;
"Plenty more Japanee diver, plenty more little brown man!"

CITY OF
DREADFUL THIRST

THE stranger came from Narromine and made his little joke;
"They say we folks in Narromine are narrow-minded folk;
But all the smartest men down here are puzzled to define
A kind of new phenomenon that came to Narromine.

"Last summer up in Narromine 'twas gettin' rather warm—
Two hundred in the water-bag, and lookin' like a storm—
We all were in the private bar, the coolest place in town,
When out across the stretch of plain a cloud came rollin' down.

"We don't respect the clouds up there, they fill us with disgust,
They mostly bring a Bogan shower—three raindrops and some dust;
But each man, simultaneous-like, to each man said, 'I think
That cloud suggests it's up to us to have another drink!'

"There's clouds of rain and clouds of dust—we'd heard of them
        before,
And sometimes in the daily press we read of 'clouds of war'.
But—if this ain't the Gospel truth I hope that I may burst—
That cloud that came to Narromine was just a cloud of thirst.

"It wasn't like a common cloud, 'twas more a sort of haze;
It settled down about the street, and stopped for days and days;
And not a drop of dew could fall, and not a sunbeam shine
To pierce that dismal sort of mist that hung on Narromine.

"Oh, Lord! we had a dreadful time beneath that cloud of thirst!
We all chucked-up our daily work and went upon the burst.
The very blacks about the town, that used to cadge for grub,
They made an organized attack and tried to loot the pub.

"We couldn't leave the private bar no matter how we tried;
Shearers and squatters, union-men and blacklegs side by side
Were drinkin' there and dursn't move, for each was sure, he said,
Before he'd get a half-a-mile the thirst would strike him dead!

"We drank until the drink gave out; we searched from room to room,
And round the pub, like drunken ghosts, went howling through
        the gloom.
The shearers found some kerosene and settled down again,
But all the squatter chaps and I, we staggered to the train.

"And once outside the cloud of thirst we felt as right as pie,
But while we stopped about the town we had to drink or die.
I hear today it's safe enough; I'm going back to work
Because they say the cloud of thirst has shifted on to Bourke.

"But when you see those clouds about—like this one over here—
All white and frothy at the top, just like a pint of beer,
It's time to go and have a drink, for if that cloud should burst
You'd find the drink would all be gone, for that's a cloud of thirst!"

.   .   .   .   .   .

We stood the man from Narromine a pint of half-and-half;
He drank it off without a gasp in one tremendous quaff;
"I joined some friends last night," he said, "in what *they* called a
    spree;
But after Narromine 'twas just a holiday to me.

And now beyond the Western Range, where sunset skies are red,
And clouds of dust, and clouds of thirst, go drifting overhead,
The railway-train is taking back, along the Western Line,
That narrow-minded person on his road to Narromine.

SALTBUSH BILL'S
GAMECOCK

'Twas Saltbush Bill, with his travelling sheep, was making his way
    to town;
He crossed them over the Hard Times Run, and he came to the
    Take 'Em Down;
He counted through at the boundary gate, and camped at the
    drafting yard:
For Stingy Smith, of the Hard Times Run, had hunted him rather
    hard.
He bore no malice to Stingy Smith—'twas simply the hand of Fate
That caused his waggon to swerve aside and shatter old Stingy's gate;
And being only the hand of Fate, it follows, without a doubt,
It wasn't the fault of Saltbush Bill that Stingy's sheep got out.
So Saltbush Bill, with an easy heart, prepared for what might befall,
Commenced his stages on Take 'Em Down, the station of Rooster
    Hall.

'Tis strange how often the men out back will take to some curious
    craft,
Some ruling passion to keep their thoughts away from the overdraft:
And Rooster Hall, of the Take 'Em Down, was widely known to fame
As breeder of champion fighting cocks—his *forte* was the British
    Game.

The passing stranger within his gates that camped with old Rooster
    Hall
Was forced to talk about fowls all night, or else not talk at all.
Though droughts should come, and though sheep should die, his
    fowls were his sole delight;
He left his shed in the flood of work to watch two game-cocks fight.
He held in scorn the Australian Game, that long-legged child of sin;
In a desperate fight, with the steel-tipped spurs, the British game
    must win!
The Australian bird was a mongrel bird, with a touch of the
    jungle cock;
The want of breeding must find him out, when facing the English
    stock;
For British breeding, and British pluck, must triumph it over all—
And that was the root of the simple creed that governed old
    Rooster Hall.

.   .   .   .   .   .

'Twas Saltbush Bill to the station rode ahead of his travelling
    sheep,
And sent a message to Rooster Hall that wakened him out of his
    sleep—
A crafty message that fetched him out, and hurried him as he
    came—
"A drover has an Australian bird to match with your British Game."
'Twas done, and done in half a trice; a five-pound note a side;
Old Rooster Hall, with his champion bird, and the drover's bird
    untried.

"Steel spurs, of course?" said old Rooster Hall; "you'll need 'em,
    without a doubt!"
"You stick the spurs on your bird!" said Bill, "but mine fights best
    without."
"Fights best without?" said old Rooster Hall; "he can't fight best
    unspurred!
You must be crazy!" But Saltbush Bill said, "Wait till you see my
    bird!"
So Rooster Hall to his fowl-yard went, and quickly back he came,
Bearing a clipt and a shaven cock, the pride of his English Game;
With an eye as fierce as an eaglehawk, and a crow like a trumpet
    call,
He strutted about on the garden walk, and cackled at Rooster
    Hall.
Then Rooster Hall sent off a boy with a word to his cronies two,
McCrae (the boss of the Black Police) and Father Donahoo.

Full many a cockfight old McCrae had held in his empty Court,
With Father D. as the picker-up—a regular all-round Sport!
They got the message of Rooster Hall, and down to his run they
    came,
Prepared to scoff at the drover's bird, and to bet on the English
    Game;
They hied them off to the drover's camp, while Saltbush rode
    before—
Old Rooster Hall was a blithsome man, when he thought of the
    treat in store.
They reached the camp, where the drover's cook, with countenance
    all serene,
Was boiling beef in an iron pot, but never a fowl was seen.

"Take off the beef from the fire," said Bill, "and wait till you see
        the fight;
There's something fresh for the bill-of-fare—there's game-fowl stew
        tonight!
For Mister Hall has a fighting cock, all feathered and clipped and
        spurred;
And he's fetched him here, for a bit of sport, to fight our Australian
        bird.
I've made a match that our pet will win, though he's hardly a
        fighting cock,
But he's game enough, and it's many a mile that he's tramped with
        the travelling stock."
The cook he banged on a saucepan lid; and, soon as the sound was
        heard,
Under the dray, in the shallow hid, a something moved and
        stirred:
A great tame emu strutted out. Said Saltbush, "Here's our bird!"
But Rooster Hall, and his cronies two, drove home without a
        word.

The passing stranger within his gates that camps with old Rooster
        Hall
Must talk about something else than fowls, if he wishes to talk
        at all.
For the record lies in the local Court, and filed in its deepest vault,
That Peter Hall, of the Take 'Em Down, was tried for a fierce
        assault
On a stranger man, who, in all good faith, and prompted by what
        he heard,
Had asked old Hall if a British Game could beat an Australian bird;
And Old McCrae, who was on the Bench, as soon as the case
        was tried,
Remarked, "Discharged with a clean discharge—the assault was
        justified!"

HAY AND HELL AND BOOLIGAL

"You come and see me, boys," he said;
"You'll find a welcome and a bed
　And whisky any time you call;
Although our township hasn't got
The name of quite a lively spot—
　You see, I live in Booligal.

"And people have an awful down
Upon the district and the town—
　Which worse than hell itself the call;
In fact, the saying far and wide
Along the Riverina side
　Is 'Hay and Hell and Booligal'.

"No doubt it suits 'em very well
To say its worse than Hay or Hell,
　But don't you heed their talk at all;
Of course, there's heat—no one denies—
And sand and dust and stacks of flies,
　And rabbits, too, at Booligal.

"But such a pleasant, quiet place—
You never see a stranger's face;
　They hardly ever care to call;
The drovers mostly pass it by—
They reckon that they'd rather die
　Than spend the night in Booligal.

"The big mosquitoes frighten some—
You'll lie awake to hear 'em hum—
　And snakes about the township crawl;
But shearers, when they get their cheque,
They never come along and wreck
　The blessed town of Booligal.

"But down to Hay the shearers come
And fill themselves with fighting-rum,
　And chase blue devils up the wall,
And fight the snaggers every day,
Until there is the deuce to pay—
　There's none of that in Booligal.

122

"Of course, there isn't much to see—
The billiard-table used to be
    The great attraction for us all,
Until some careless, drunken curs
Got sleeping on it in their spurs,
    And ruined it, in Booligal.

"Just now there is a howling drought
That pretty near has starved us out—
    It never seems to rain at all;
But, if there *should* come any rain,
You couldn't cross the black-soil plain—
    You'd have to stop in Booligal."

.   .   .   .   .

"We'd have to stop!" With bated breath
We prayed that both in life and death
    Our fate in other lines might fall:
"Oh, send us to our just reward
In Hay or Hell, but, gracious Lord,
    Deliver us from Booligal!"

A WALGETT
EPISODE

THE sun strikes down with a blinding glare;
  The skies are blue and the plains are wide,
The saltbush plains that are burnt and bare
  By Walgett out on the Barwon side—
The Barwon River that wanders down
In a leisurely manner by Walgett Town.

There came a stranger—a "Cockatoo"—
  The word means farmer, as all men know,
Who dwell in the land where the kangaroo
  Barks loud at dawn, and the white-eyed crow
Uplifts his song on the stock-yard fence
As he watches the lambkins passing hence.

The sunburnt stranger was gaunt and brown,
  But it soon appeared that he meant to flout
The iron law of the country town,
  Which is—that the stranger has got to shout:
"If he will not shout we must take him down,"
Remarked the yokels of Walgett Town.

They baited a trap with a crafty bait,
  With a crafty bait, for they held discourse
Concerning a new chum who there of late
  Had bought such a thoroughly lazy horse;
They would wager that no one could ride him down
The length of the city of Walgett Town.

The stranger was born on a horse's hide;
  So he took the wagers, and made them good
With his hard-earned cash—but his hopes they died,
  For the horse was a clothes-horse, made of wood!—
'Twas a well-known horse that had taken down
Full many a stranger in Walgett Town.

The stranger smiled with a sickly smile—
  'Tis a sickly smile that the loser grins—
And he said he had travelled for quite a while
  A-trying to sell some marsupial skins.
"And I thought that perhaps, as you've took me down,
You would buy them from me, in Walgett Town!"

He said that his home was at Wingadee,
    At Wingadee, where he had for sale
Some fifty skins and would guarantee
    They were full-sized skins, with the ears and tail
Complete; and he sold them for money down
To a venturesome buyer in Walgett Town.

Then he smiled a smile as he pouched the pelf,
    "I'm glad that I'm quit of them, win or lose:
You can fetch them in when it suits yourself,
    And you'll find the skins—on the kangaroos!"
Then he left—and the silence settled down
Like a tangible thing upon Walgett Town.

FATHER RILEY'S HORSE

'TWAS the horse thief, Andy Regan, that was hunted like a dog
    By the troopers of the Upper Murray side;
They had searched in every gully, they had looked in every log
    But never sight or track of him they spied,
Till the priest at Kiley's Crossing heard a knocking very late
    And a whisper "Father Riley—come across!"
So his Reverence, in pyjamas, trotted softly to the gate
    And admitted Andy Regan—and a horse!

"Now, it's listen, Father Riley, to the words I've got to say,
    For it's close upon my death I am tonight.
With the troopers hard behind me I've been hiding all the day
    In the gullies keeping close and out of sight.
But they're watching all the ranges till there's not a bird could fly,
    And I'm fairly worn to pieces with the strife,
So I'm taking no more trouble, but I'm going home to die,
    'Tis the only way I see to save my life.

"Yes, I'm making home to mother's, and I'll die o' Tuesday next
    An' buried on the Thursday—and, of course,
I'm prepared to do my penance; but with one thing I'm perplexed
    And it's—Father, it's this jewel of a horse!
He was never bought nor paid for, and there's not a man can swear
    To his owner or his breeder, but I know
That his sire was by Pedantic from the Old Pretender mare,
    And his dam was close related to The Roe.

"And there's nothing in the district that can race him for a step—
    He could canter while they're going at their top:
He's the king of all the leppers that was ever seen to lep;
    A five-foot fence—he'd clear it in a hop!
So I'll leave him with you, Father, till the dead shall rise again,
    'Tis yourself that knows a good un; and, of course,
You can say he's got by Moonlight out of Paddy Murphy's plain
    If you're ever asked the breeding of the horse!

"But it's getting on to daylight, and it's time to say good-bye,
  For the stars above the East are growing pale.
And I'm making home to mother—and it's hard for me to die!
  But it's harder still, is keeping out of gaol!
You can ride the old horse over to my grave across the dip,
  Where the wattle-bloom is waving overhead.
Sure he'll jump them fences easy—you must never raise the whip
  Or he'll rush 'em!—now, good-bye!" and he had fled!

So they buried Andy Regan, and they buried him to rights,
  In the graveyard at the back of Kiley's Hill;
There were five-and-twenty mourners who had five-and-twenty fights
  Till the very boldest fighters had their fill.
There were fifty horses racing from the graveyard to the pub.
  And the riders flogged each other all the while—
And the lashins of the liquor! And the lavins of the grub!
  Oh, poor Andy went to rest in proper style.

Then the races came to Kiley's—with a steeple chase and all,
  For the folk were mostly Irish round about,
And it takes an Irish rider to be fearless of a fall;
  They were training morning in and morning out.
But they never started training till the sun was on the course,
  For a superstitious story kept 'em back.
That the ghost of Andy Regan on a slashing chestnut horse
  Had been training by the starlight on the track.

And they read the nominations for the races with surprise
  And amusement at the Father's little joke,
For a novice had been entered for the steeplechasing prize,
  And they found that it was Father Riley's moke!
He was neat enough to gallop, he was strong enough to stay!
  But his owner's views of training were immense,
For the Reverend Father Riley used to ride him every day,
  And he never saw a hurdle nor a fence.

And the priest would join the laughter; "Oh," said he, "I put him in,
  For there's five-and-twenty sovereigns to be won;
And the poor would find it useful if the chestnut chanced to win,
  As he'll maybe do when all is said and done!"
He had called him Faugh-a-ballagh (which is French for 'Clear
      the course'),
  And his colours were a vivid shade of green:
All the Dooleys and O'Donnells were on Father Riley's horse,
  While the Orangeman were backing Mandarin!

It was Hogan, the dog-poisoner—aged man and very wise,
    Who was camping in the racecourse with his swag,
And who ventured the opinion, to the township's great surprise,
    That the race would go to Father Riley's nag.
"You can talk about your riders—and the horse has not been
        schooled,
    And the fences is terrific, and the rest!
When the field is fairly going, then ye'll see ye've all been fooled.
    And the chestnut horse will battle with the best.

"For there's some has got condition, and they think the race is
        sure,
    And the chestnut horse will fall beneath the weight;
But the hopes of all the helpless, and the prayers of all the poor,
    Will be running by his side to keep him straight.
And it's what the need of schoolin' or of workin' on the track,
    Whin the Saints are there to guide him round the course!
I've prayed him over every fence—I've prayed him out and back!
    And I'll bet my cash on Father Riley's horse!"

                    .   .   .   .   .

Oh, the steeple was a caution! They went tearin' round and round,
    And the fences rang and rattled where they struck.
There was some that cleared the water—there was more fell in and
        drowned—
    Some blamed the men and others blamed the luck!
But the whips were flying freely when the field came into view
    For the finish down the long green stretch of course,
And in front of all the flyers, jumpin' like a kangaroo,
    Came the rank outsider—Father Riley's horse!

Oh, the shouting and the cheering as he rattled past the post!
    For he left the others standing, in the straight;
And the rider—well, they reckoned it was Andy Regan's ghost,
    And it beat 'em how a ghost would draw the weight!
But he weighed in, nine stone seven; then he laughed and dis-
        appeared,
    Like a Banshee (which is Spanish for an elf),
And old Hogan muttered sagely, "If it wasn't for the beard
    They'd be thinking it was Andy Regan's self!"

And the poor at Kiley's Crossing drank the health at Christmastide
   Of the chestnut and his rider dressed in green.
There was never such a rider, not since Andy Regan died,
   And they wondered who on earth he could have been,
But they settled it among 'em, for the story got about,
   'Mongst the bushmen and the people on the course,
That the Devil had been ordered to let Andy Regan out
   For the steeplechase on Father Riley's horse!

THE
SCOTTISH ENGINEER

WITH eyes that searched in the dark,
Peering along the line,
Stood the grim Scotsman, Hector Clark,
Driver of "Forty-nine".
And the veldt-fire flamed on the hills ahead,
Like a blood-red beacon sign.

There was word of a fight to the north,
And a column too hardly pressed,
So they started the Highlanders forth,
Heedless of food or rest.

But the pipers gaily played,
Chanting their fierce delight,
And the armoured carriages rocked and swayed,
Laden with men of the Scots Brigade,
Hurrying up to the fight,
And the grim, grey Highland engineer
Driving them into the night.

Then a signal light glowed red,
And a picket came to the track.
"Enemy holding the line ahead;
Three of our mates we have left for dead,
Only we two got back."
And far to the north through the still night air
They heard the rifles crack.

And the boom of a gun rang out,
Like the sound of a deep appeal,
And the picket stood in doubt
By the side of the driving-wheel.

But the engineer looked down,
With his hand on the starting-bar,
"Ride ye back to the town,
Ye know what my orders are,
Maybe they're wanting the Scots Brigade
Up on those hills afar.

"I am no soldier at all,
Only an engineer;
But I could not bear that the folk should say
Over in Scotland—Glasgow way—
That Hector Clark stayed here
With the Scots Brigade till the foe was gone,
With ever a rail to run her on.
Ready behind! Stand clear!

"Fireman, get you gone
Into the armoured train—
I will drive her alone;
One more trip—and perhaps the last—
With a well-raked fire and an open blast;
Hark to the rifles again!"

.   .   .   .   .   .

On through the choking dark,
Never a lamp nor a light,
Never an engine spark
Showing her hurried flight,
Over the lonely plain
Rushed the great armoured train,
Hurrying up to the fight.

Then with her living freight
On to the foe she came,
And the rifles snapped their hate.
And the darkness spouted flame.

Over the roar of the fray
The hungry bullets whined,
As she dashed through the foe that lay
Loading and firing blind,
Till the glare of the furnace, burning clear,
Showed them the form of the engineer

Sharply and well defined.
Through! They are safely through!
Hark to the column's cheer!
Surely the driver knew
He was to halt her here;
But he took no heed of the signals red,
And the fireman found, when he climbed ahead,
There on the floor of his engine—dead—
The Scottish Engineer!

131

SONG OF
THE FUTURE

'Tis strange that in a land so strong
So strong and bold in mighty youth,
We have no poet's voice of truth
To sing for us a wondrous song.

Our chiefest singer yet has sung
In wild, sweet notes a passing strain,
All carelessly and sadly flung
To that dull world he thought so vain.

"I care for nothing, good nor bad,
My hopes are gone, my pleasures fled,
I am but sifting sand," he said:
What wonder Gordon's songs were sad!

And yet, not always sad and hard;
In cheerful mood and light of heart
He told the tale of Britomarte,
And wrote the Rhyme of Joyous Garde.

And some have said that Nature's face
To us is always sad; but these
Have never felt the smiling grace
Of waving grass and forest trees
On sunlit plains as wide as seas.

"A land where dull Despair is king
O'er scentless flower and songless bird!"
But we have heard the bell-birds ring
Their silver bells at eventide,
Like fairies on the mountain side,
The sweetest note man ever heard.

The wild thrush lifts a note of mirth;
The bronzewing pigeons call and coo
Beside their nests the long day through;
The magpie warbles clear and strong
A joyous, glad, thanksgiving song,
For all God's mercies upon earth.

And many voices such as these
Are joyful sounds for those to tell,
Who know the Bush and love it well,
With all its hidden mysteries.

We cannot love the restless sea,
That rolls and tosses to and fro
Like some fierce creature in its glee;
For human weal or human woe
It has no touch of sympathy.

For us the bush is never sad:
Its myriad voices whisper low,
In tones the bushmen only know,
Its sympathy and welcome glad.
For us the roving breezes bring
From many a blossum-tufted tree—
Where wild bees murmur dreamily—
The honey-laden breath of Spring.

   .   .   .   .   .

We have our tales of other days,
Good tales the northern wanderers tell
When bushmen meet and camp-fires blaze,
And round the ring of dancing light
The great, dark bush with arms of night
Folds every hearer in its spell.

We have our songs—not songs of strife
And hot blood spilt on sea and land;
But lilts that link achievement grand
To honest toil and valiant life.

Lift ye your faces to the sky
Ye barrier mountains in the west
Who lie so peacefully at rest
Enshrouded in a haze of blue;
'Tis hard to feel that years went by
Before the pioneers broke through
Your rocky heights and walls of stone,
And made your secrets all their own.

For years the fertile Western plains
Were hid behind your sullen walls,
Your cliffs and crags and waterfalls
All weatherworn with tropic rains.

133

Between the mountains and the sea
Like Israelites with staff in hand,
The people waited restlessly:
They looked towards the mountains old
And saw the sunsets come and go
With gorgeous golden afterglow,
That made the West a fairyland,
And marvelled what that West might be
Of which such wondrous tales were told.

For tales were told of inland seas
Like sullen oceans, salt and dead,
And sandy deserts, white and wan,
Where never trod the foot of man,
Nor bird went winging overhead,
Nor ever stirred a gracious breeze
To wake the silence with its breath—
A land of loneliness and death.

At length the hardy pioneers
By rock and crag found out the way,
And woke with voices of today
A silence kept for years and years.

Upon the Western slope they stood
And saw—a wide expanse of plain
As far as eye could stretch or see
Go rolling westward endlessly.
The native grasses, tall as grain,
Bowed, waved and rippled in the breeze;
From boughs of blossom-laden trees
The parrots answered back again.
They saw the land that it was good,
A land of fatness all untrod,
And gave their silent thanks to God.

The way is won! The way is won!
And straightway from the barren coast
There came a westward-marching host,
That aye and ever onward prest
With eager faces to the West,
Along the pathway of the sun.

The mountains saw them marching by:
They faced the all-consuming drought,
They would not rest in settled land:
But, taking each his life in hand,
Their faces ever westward bent
Beyond the farthest settlement,
Responding to the challenge cry
Of "better country farther out".

And lo, a miracle! the land
But yesterday was all unknown,
The wild man's boomerang was thrown
Where now great busy cities stand.
It was not much, you say, that these
Should win their way where none withstood;
In sooth there was not much of blood—
No war was fought between the seas.

It was not much! but we who know
The strange capricious land they trod—
At times a stricken, parching sod,
At times with raging floods beset—
Through which they found their lonely way
Are quite content that you should say
It was not much, while we can feel
That nothing in the ages old,
In song or story written yet
On Grecian urn or Roman arch,
Though it should ring with clash of steel,
Could braver histories unfold
Than this bush story, yet untold—
The story of their westward march.

.   .   .   .   .   .

But times are changed, and changes rung
From old to new—the olden days,
The old bush life and all its ways,
Are passing from us all unsung.
The freedom, and the hopeful sense
Of toil that brought due recompense,
Of room for all, has passed away,
And lies forgotten with the dead.
Within our streets men cry for bread

In cities built but yesterday.
About us stretches wealth of land,
A boundless wealth of virgin soil
As yet unfruitful and untilled!
Our willing workmen, strong and skilled,
Within our cities idle stand,
And cry aloud for leave to toil.

The stunted children come and go
In squalid lanes and alleys black:
We follow but the beaten track
Of other nations, and we grow
In wealth for some—for many, woe.

And it may be that we who live
In this new land apart, beyond
The hard old world grown fierce and fond
And bound by precedent and bond,
May read the riddle right, and give
New hope to those who dimly see
That all things yet shall be for good,
And teach the world at length to be
One vast united brotherhood.

   .   .   .   .   .   .

So may it be! and he who sings
In accents hopeful, clear, and strong,
The glories which that future brings
Shall sing, indeed, a wondrous song.

ANTHONY CONSIDINE

Out in the wastes of the West countrie,
    Out where the white stars shine,
Grim and silent as such men be,
Rideth a man with a history—
    Anthony Considine.

For the ways of men they are manifold
    As their differing views in life;
Some sell themselves for the lust of gold,
    And some for the lust of strife:
But this man counted the world well lost
    For the love of his neighbour's wife.

They fled together, as those must flee
    Whom all men hold in blame;
Each to the other must all things be
Who cross the gulf of iniquity
    And live in the land of shame.

But a light-o'-love, if she sins with one,
    She sinneth with ninety-nine:
The rule holds good since the world begun—
Since ever the streams began to run
    And the stars began to shine.
The rule holds still, and he found it true—
    Anthony Considine.

A nobler spirit had turned in scorn
    From a love that was stained with mire;
A weaker being might mourn and mourn
    For the loss of his Heart's Desire:
But the anger of Anthony Considine
    Blazed up like a flaming fire.

And she, with her new love, presently
    Came past with her eyes ashine;
And God so willed it, and God knows why,
She turned and laughed as they passed him by—
    Anthony Considine.

Her laughter stung as a whip might sting;
   And mad with his wounded pride
He turned and sprang with a panther's spring
   And struck at his rival's side:
And only the woman, shuddering,
   Could tell how the dead man died!

She dared not speak—and the mystery
   Is buried in auld lang syne,
But out on the wastes of the West countrie,
Grim and silent as such men be,
Rideth a man with a history—
   Anthony Considine.

SONG OF
THE ARTESIAN WATER

Now the stock have started dying, for the Lord has sent a drought;
But we're sick of prayers and Providence—we're going to do without;
With the derricks up above us and the solid earth below,
We are waiting at the lever for the word to let her go.
   Sinking down, deeper down,
   Oh, we'll sink it deeper down:
As the drill is plugging downward at a thousand feet of level,
If the Lord won't send us water, oh, we'll get it from the devil;
Yes, we'll get it from the devil deeper down.

Now, our engine's built in Glasgow by a very canny Scot,
And he marked it twenty horse-power, but he don't know what
  is what:
When Canadian Bill is firing with the sun-dried gidgee logs,
She can equal thirty horses and a score or so of dogs.
   Sinking down, deeper down,
   Oh, we're going deeper down:
If we fail to get the water, then it's ruin to the squatter,
For the drought is on the station and the weather's growing hotter,
But we're bound to get the water deeper down.

But the shaft has started caving and the sinking's very slow,
And the yellow rods are bending in the water down below,
And the tubes are always jamming, and they can't be made to
  shift
Till we nearly burst the engine with a forty horse-power lift.
   Sinking down, deeper down,
   Oh, we're going deeper down:
Though the shaft is always caving, and the tubes are always
  jamming,
Yet we'll fight our way to water while the stubborn drill is
  ramming—
While the stubborn drill is ramming deeper down.

But there's no artesian water, though we've passed three thousand
  feet,
And the contract price is growing, and the boss is nearly. beat.
But it must be down beneath us, and it's down we've got to go,
Though she's bumping on the solid rock four thousand feet below.

139

Sinking down, deeper down,
Oh, we're going deeper down:
And it's time they heard us knocking on the roof of Satan's dwellin';
But we'll get artesian water if we cave the roof of hell in—
Oh! we'll get artesian water deeper down.

But it's hark! the whistle's blowing with a wild, exultant blast,
And the boys are madly cheering, for they've struck the flow at
    last;
And it's rushing up the tubing from four thousand feet below,
Till it spouts above the casing in a million-gallon flow.
And it's down, deeper down—
Oh, it comes from deeper down;
It is flowing, ever flowing, in a free, unstinted measure
From the silent hidden places where the old earth hides her
    treasure—
Where the old earth hides her treasures deeper down.

And it's clear away the timber, and it's let the water run:
How it glimmers in the shadow, how it flashes in the sun!
By the silent belts of timber, by the miles of blazing plain
It is bringing hope and comfort to the thirsty land again.
Flowing down, further down;
It is flowing further down
To the tortured thirsty cattle, bringing gladness in its going;
Through the droughty days of summer it is flowing, ever flowing—
It is flowing, ever flowing, further down.

A DISQUALIFIED
JOCKEY'S STORY

You see, the thing was this way—there was me,
That rode Panoppoly, the Splendor mare,
And Ikey Chambers on the Iron Dook,
And Smith, the half-caste rider on Regret,
And that long bloke from Wagga—him that rode
Veronikew, the Snowy River horse.
Well, none of them had chances—not a chance
Among the lot, unless the rest fell dead
Or wasn't trying—for a blind man's dog
Could see Enchantress was a certain cop,
And all the books was layin' six to four.

They brought her out to show our lot the road,
Or so they said: but, then Gord's truth! you know,
You can't believe 'em, though they took an oath
On forty Bibles that they'd tell the truth.
But anyhow, an amateur was up
On this Enchantress; and so Ike and me,
We thought that we might frighten him a bit
By asking if he minded riding rough—
"Oh, not at all," says he, "oh, not at all!
I learnt at Robbo Park, and if it comes
To bumping I'm your Moses! Strike me blue!"

Says he, "I'll bump you over either rail,
The inside rail or outside—which you choose
Is good enough for me"—which settled Ike.
For he was shaky since he near got killed
From being sent a buster on the rail,
When some chap bumped his horse and fetched him down
At Stony Bridge; so Ikey thought it best
To leave this bloke alone, and I agreed.

So all the books was layin' six to four
Against the favourite, and the amateur
Was walking this Enchantress up and down,
And me and Smithy backed him; for we thought
We might as well get something for ourselves,

Because we knew our horses couldn't win.
But Ikey wouldn't back him for a bob;
Because he said he reckoned he was stiff,
And all the books was layin' six to four.

Well, anyhow, before the start the news
Got around that this here amateur was stiff,
And our good stuff was blued, and all the books
Was in it, and the prices lengthened out,
And every book was bustin' of his throat,
And layin' five to one the favourite.
So there was we that couldn't win ourselves,
And this here amateur that wouldn't try,
And all the books was layin' five to one.

So Smithy says to me, "You take a hold
Of that there moke of yours, and round the turn
Come up behind Enchantress with the whip
And let her have it; that long bloke and me
Will wait ahead, and when she comes to us
We'll pass her on and belt her down the straight,
And Ikey'll flog her home—because his boss
Is judge and steward and the Lord knows what,
And so he won't be touched; and, as for us,
We'll swear we only hit her by mistake!"
And all the books was layin' five to one.

Well, off we went, and comin' to the turn
I saw the amateur was holding back
And poking into every hole he could
To get her blocked; and so I pulled behind
And drew the whip and dropped it on the mare.
I let her have it twice, and then she shot
Ahead of me, and Smithy opened out
And let her up beside him on the rails,
And kept her there a-beltin' her like smoke
Until she struggled past him, pullin' hard,
And came to Ike; but Ikey drew his whip
And hit her on the nose, and sent her back
And won the race himself—for, after all,
It seems he had a fiver on The Dook
And never told us—so our stuff was lost.
And then they had us up for ridin' foul,

And warned us off the tracks for twelve months each
To get our livin' any way we could;
But Ikey wasn't touched, because his boss
Was judge and steward and the Lord knows what.

But Mister—if you'll lend us half-a-crown,
I know three certain winners at the Park—
Three certain cops as no one knows but me;
And—thank you, Mister, come an' have a beer
(I always like a beer about this time) . . .
Well, so long, Mister, till we meet again.

THE ROAD
TO GUNDAGAI

THE mountain road goes up and down
From Gundagai to Tumut Town.

And, branching off, there runs a track
Across the foothills grim and black,

Across the plains and ranges grey
To Sydney city far away.

  .   .   .   .   .

It came by chance one day that I
From Tumut rode to Gundagai,

And reached about the evening tide
The crossing where the roads divide;

And, waiting at the crossing place,
I saw a maiden fair of face,

With eyes of deepest violet blue,
And cheeks to match the rose in hue—

The fairest maids Australia knows
Are bred among the mountain snows.

Then, fearing I might go astray,
I asked if she could show the way.

Her voice might well a man bewitch—
Its tones so supple, deep, and rich.

"The tracks are clear," she made reply,
"And this goes down to Sydney town,
And that one goes to Gundagai."

Then slowly, looking coyly back,
She went along the Sydney track

"With French to Kimberley"—
the frontispiece Hal Gye prepared for *Rio Grande*

And I for one was well content
To go the road the lady went;

But round the turn a swain she met—
The kiss she gave him haunts me yet!

   .   .   .   .   .   .

I turned and travelled with a sigh
The lonely road to Gundagai.

SALTBUSH BILL'S
SECOND FIGHT

THE news came down on the Castlereagh, and went to the world
      at large,
That twenty thousand travelling sheep, with Saltbush Bill in charge,
Were drifting down from a dried-out run to ravage the Castlereagh;
And the squatters swore when they heard the news, and wished
      they were well away:
For the name and the fame of Saltbush Bill were over the country-
      side
For the wonderful way that he fed his sheep, and the dodges and
      tricks he tried.
He would lose his way on a Main Stock Route, and stray to the
      squatters' grass;
He would come to a run with the boss away, and swear he had
      leave to pass;
And back of all and behind it all, as well the squatters knew,
If he had to fight, he would fight all day, so long as his sheep
      got through:
But this is the story of Stingy Smith, the owner of Hard Times Hill,
And the way that he chanced on a fighting man to reckon with
      Saltbush Bill.

     .   .   .   .   .   .

'Twas Stingy Smith on his stockyard sat, and prayed for an early
      Spring,
When he started at sight of a clean-shaved tramp, who walked with
      a jaunty swing;
For a clean-shaved tramp with a jaunty walk a-swinging along the
      track
Is as rare a thing as a feathered frog on the desolate roads out back.
So the tramp he made for the travellers' hut, to ask could he camp
      the night;
But Stingy Smith had a bright idea, and called to him,
  "Can you fight?"

"Why, what's the game?" said the clean-shaved tramp, as he looked
      at him up and down;
"If you want a battle, get off that fence, and I'll kill you for
      half-a-crown!
But, Boss, you'd better not fight with me—it wouldn't be fair nor
      right;

146

I'm Stiffener Joe, from the Rocks Brigade, and I killed a man in
    a fight:
I served two years for it, fair and square, and now I'm a-trampin'
    back,
To look for a peaceful quiet life away on the outside track."

"Oh, it's not myself, but a drover chap," said Stingy Smith with glee
"A bullying fellow called Saltbush Bill, and you are the man for me.
He's on the road with his hungry sheep, and he's certain to raise
    a row,
For he's bullied the whole of the Castlereagh till he's got them
    under cow—
Just pick a quarrel and raise a fight, and leather him good and hard,
And I'll take good care that his wretched sheep don't wander a
    half a yard.
It's a five-pound job if you belt him well—do anything short of kill,
For there isn't a beak on the Castlereagh will fine you for Saltbush
    Bill."

"I'll take the job," said the fighting man; "and, hot as this cove
    appears,
He'll stand no chance with a bloke like me, what's lived on the
    game for years;
For he's maybe learnt in a boxing school, and sparred for a round
    or so,
But I've fought all hands in a ten-foot ring each night in a travelling
    show;
They earned a pound if they stayed three rounds, and they tried for
    it every night.
In a ten-foot ring! Oh, that's the game that teaches a bloke to fight,
For they'd rush and clinch—it was Dublin Rules, and we drew
    no colour line;
And they all tried hard for to earn the pound, but they got no
    pound of mine.
If I saw no chance in the opening round I'd slog at their wind,
    and wait
Till an opening came—and it *always* came—and I settled 'em, sure
    as fate;
Left on the ribs and right on the jaw—and, when the chance
    comes, make sure!
And it's there a professional bloke like me gets home on an amateur:
For it's my experience every day, and I make no doubt it's yours,

That a third-class pro is an over-match for the best of the
    amateurs———"
"Oh, take your swag to the travellers' hut," said Smith, "for you
    waste your breath;
You've a first-class chance, if you lose the fight, of talking your man
    to death.
I'll tell the cook you're to have your grub, and see that you eat
    your fill,
And come to the scratch all fit and well to leather this Saltbush
    Bill."

       .   .   .   .   .   .

'Twas Saltbush Bill, and his travelling sheep were wending their
    weary way
On the Main Stock Route, through the Hard Times Run, on their
    six-mile stage a day;
And he strayed a mile from the Main Stock Route, and started to
    feed along,
And when Stingy Smith came up Bill said that the Route was
    surveyed wrong;
And he tried to prove that the sheep had rushed and strayed from
    their camp at night,
But the fighting man he kicked Bill's dog, and of course that
    meant a fight.

So they sparred and fought, and they shifted ground, and never
    a sound was heard
But the thudding fists on their brawny ribs, and the seconds'
    muttered word,
Till the fighting man shot home his left on the ribs with a mighty
    clout,
And his right flashed up with a half-arm blow—and Saltbush Bill
    "went out".
He fell face down, and towards the blow; and their hearts with
    fear were filled,
For he lay as still as a fallen tree, and they thought that he must
    be killed.

So Stingy Smith and the fighting man, they lifted him from the
    ground,
And sent back home for a brandy-flask, and they slowly fetched him
    round;

But his head was bad, and his jaw was hurt—in fact, he could
    scarcely speak—
So they let him spell till he got his wits; and he camped on the
    run a week,
While the travelling sheep went here and there, wherever they
    liked to stray,
Till Saltbush Bill was fit once more for the track to the Castlereagh.

      .   .   .   .   .   .

Then Stingy Smith he wrote a note, and gave to the fighting man:
'Twas writ to the boss of the neighbouring run, and thus the missive
    ran:
"The man with this is a fighting man, one Stiffener Joe by name;
He came near murdering Saltbush Bill, and I found it a costly game:
But it's worth your while to employ the chap, for there isn't the
    slightest doubt
You'll have no trouble from Saltbush Bill while this man hangs
    about."
But an answer came by the next week's mail, with news that might
    well appal:
"The man you sent with a note is not a fighting man at all!
He has shaved his beard, and has cut his hair, but I spotted him
    at a look;
He is Tom Devine, who has worked for years for Saltbush Bill as
    cook.
Bill coached him up in the fighting yard, and taught him the tale
    by rote,
And they shammed to fight, and they got your grass, and divided
    your five-pound note.
'Twas a clean take-in; and you'll find it wise—'twill save you a lot
    of pelf—
When next you're hiring a fighting man, just fight him a round
    yourself."

      .   .   .   .   .   .

And the teamsters out on the Castlereagh, when they meet with
    a week of rain,
And the waggon sinks to its axle-tree, deep down in the black-soil
    plain,
When the bullocks wade in a sea of mud, and strain at the load
    of wool,
And the cattle-dogs at the bullocks' heels are biting to make them
    pull,

When the off-side driver flays the team, and curses them while he
    flogs,
And the air is thick with the language used, and the clamour of
    men and dogs—
The teamsters say, as they pause to rest and moisten each hairy
    throat,
They wish they could swear like Stingy Smith when he read that
    neighbour's note.

HARD LUCK

I LEFT the course, and by my side
    There walked a ruined tout—
A hungry creature, evil-eyed,
    Who poured this story out.

"You see," he said, "there came a swell
    To Kensington today,
And, if I picked the winners well,
    A crown at least he'd pay.

"I picked three winners straight, I did;
    I filled his purse with pelf,
And then he gave me half-a-quid
    To back one for myself.

"A half-a-quid to me he cast—
    I wanted it indeed;
So help me Bob, for two days past
    I haven't had a feed.

"But still I thought my luck was in,
    I couldn't go astray—
I put it all on Little Min,
    And lost it straightaway.

"I haven't got a bite or bed,
    I'm absolutely stuck;
So keep this lesson in your head:
    Don't over-trust your luck!"

The folks went homeward, near and far,
    The tout, oh! where was he?
Ask where the empty boilers are
    Beside the Circular Quay.

SONG OF
THE FEDERATION

As the nations sat together, grimly waiting—
The fierce and ancient nations battle-scarred—
Grown grey in their lusting and their hating,
  Ever armed and ever ready keeping guard,
Through the tumult of their warlike preparation
  And the half-stilled clamour of the drums
Came a voice crying, "Lo, a new-made Nation,
  To her place in the sisterhood she comes!"

And she came. She was beautiful as morning,
  With the bloom of the roses on her mouth,
Like a young queen lavishly adorning
  Her charms with the splendours of the South.
And the fierce old nations, looking on her,
  Said, "Nay, surely she were quickly overthrown;
Hath she strength for the burden laid upon her,
  Hath she power to protect and guard her own?"

Then she spoke, and her voice was clear and ringing
  In the ears of the nations old and grey,
Saying, "Hark, and ye shall hear my children singing
  Their war-song in countries far away.
They are strangers to the tumult of the battle,
  They are few, but their hearts are very strong,
'Twas but yesterday they called unto the cattle,
  But they now sing Australia's marching song."

SONG OF THE AUSTRALIANS IN ACTION

For the honour of Australia, our Mother,
  Side by side with our kin from over sea,
We have fought and we have tested one another,
  And enrolled among the brotherhood are we.

There was never post of danger but we sought it
  In the fighting, through the fire, and through the
    flood
There was never prize so costly but we bought it,
  Though we paid for its purchase with our blood.

Was there any road too rough for us to travel?
  Was there any path too far for us to tread?
You can track us by the blood drops on the gravel
  On the roads that we milestoned with our dead!

And for you. O our young and anxious mother,
  O'er your great gains keeping watch and ward,
Neither fearing nor despising any other,
  We will hold your possessions with the sword.

.   .   .   .   .   .

Then they passed to the place of world-long sleeping,
  The grey-clad figures with their dead,
To the sound of their women softly weeping
  And the Dead March moaning at their head:

And the Nations, as the grim procession ended,
  Whispered, "Child, thou has seen the price we pay;
From War may we ever be defended,
  Kneel thee down, new-made Sister—Let us Pray!"

OLD
AUSTRALIAN WAYS

THE London lights are far abeam
  Behind a bank of cloud,
Along the shore the gaslights gleam,
  The gale is piping loud;
And down the Channel, groping blind,
  We drive her through the haze
Towards the land we left behind—
The good old land of "never mind",
  And old Australian ways.

The narrow ways of English folk
  Are not for such as we;
They bear the long-accustomed yoke
  Of staid conservancy:
But all our roads are new and strange,
  And through our blood there runs
The vagabonding love of change
That drove us westward of the range
  And westward of the suns.

The city folk go to and fro
  Behind a prison's bars,
They never feel the breezes blow
  And never see the stars;
They never hear in blossomed trees
  The music low and sweet
Of wild birds making melodies,
Nor catch the little laughing breeze
  That whispers in the wheat.

Our fathers came of roving stock
  That could not fixed abide:
And we have followed field and flock
  Since e'er we learnt to ride;
By miner's camp and shearing shed,
  In land of heat and drought,
We followed where our fortunes led,
With fortune always on ahead
  And always farther out.

The wind is in the barley-grass,
　The wattles are in bloom;
The breezes greet us as they pass
　With honey-sweet perfume;
The parakeets go screaming by
　With flash of golden wing,
And from the swamp the wild-ducks cry
Their long-drawn note of revelry,
　Rejoicing at the Spring.

So throw the weary pen aside
　And let the papers rest,
For we must saddle up and ride
　Towards the blue hill's breast:
And we must travel far and fast
　Across their rugged maze,
To find the Spring of Youth at last,
And call back from the buried past
　The old Australian ways.

When Clancy took the drover's track
　In years of long ago,
He drifted to the outer back
　Beyond the Overflow;
By rolling plain and rocky shelf,
　With stockwhip in his hand,
He reached at last (oh, lucky elf!)
The Town of Come-and-Help-Yourself
　In Rough-and-Ready Land.

And if it be that you would know
　The tracks he used to ride,
Then you must saddle up and go
　Beyond the Queensland side,
Beyond the reach of rule or law,
　To ride the long day through,
In Nature's homestead—filled with awe,
You then might see what Clancy saw
　And know what Clancy knew.

BALLAD OF
THE *CALLIOPE*

By the far Samoan shore,
Where the league-long rollers pour
All the wash of the Pacific on the coral-guarded bay,
Riding lightly at their ease,
In the calm of tropic seas,
The three great nations' warships at their anchors proudly lay.

Riding lightly, head to wind,
With the coral reefs behind,
Three German and three Yankee ships were mirrored in the blue;
And on one ship unfurled
Was the flag that rules the world—
For on the old *Calliope* the flag of England flew.

When the gentle off-shore breeze,
That had scarcely stirred the trees,
Dropped down to utter stillness, and the glass began to fall,
Away across the main
Lowered the coming hurricane,
And far away to seaward hung the cloud-wrack like a pall.

If the word had passed around,
"Let us move to safer ground;
Let us steam away to seaward"—then this tale were not to tell!
But each Captain seemed to say
"If the others stay, I stay!"
And they lingered at their moorings till the shades of evening fell.

Then the cloud-wrack neared them fast,
And there came a sudden blast,
And the hurricane came leaping down a thousand miles of main!
Like a lion on its prey,
Leapt the storm fiend on the bay,
And the vessels shook and shivered as their cables felt the strain.

As the surging seas came by,
That were running mountains high,
The vessels started dragging, drifting slowly to the lee;
And the darkness of the night
Hid the coral reefs from sight,
And the Captains dared not risk the chance to grope their way to sea.

In the dark they dared not shift!
They were forced to wait and drift;
All hands stood by uncertain would the anchors hold or no.
But the men on deck could see,
If a chance for them might be,
There was little chance of safety for the men who were below.

Through that long, long night of dread,
While the storm raged overhead,
They were waiting by their engines, with the furnace fires aroar;
So they waited, staunch and true,
Though they knew, and well they knew,
They must drown like rats imprisoned if the vessel touched the
        shore.

When the grey dawn broke at last,
And the long, long night was past,
While the hurricane redoubled, lest its prey should steal away,
On the rocks, all smashed and strown,
Were the German vessels thrown,
While the Yankees, swamped and helpless, drifted shorewards down
        the bay.

Then at last spoke Captain Kane,
"All our anchors are in vain,
And the Germans and the Yankees they have drifted to the lee!
Cut the cables at the bow!
We must trust the engines now!
Give her steam, and let her have it, lads! we'll fight her out to sea!"

And the answer came with cheers
From the stalwart engineers,
From the grim and grimy firemen at the furnaces below;
And above the sullen roar
Of the breakers on the shore
Came the throbbing of the engines as they laboured to and fro.

If the strain should find a flaw,
Should a bolt or rivet draw,
Then—God help them! for the vessel were a plaything in the tide!
With a face of honest cheer
Quoth an English engineer,
"I will answer for the engines that were built on old Thames-side!

"For the stays and stanchions taut,
For the rivets truly wrought,
For the valves that fit their faces as a glove should fit the hand.
Give her every ounce of power;
If we make a knot an hour
Then it's way enough to steer her, and we'll drive her from the land."

Life a foam-flake tossed and thrown,
She could barely hold her own,
While the other ships all helplessly were drifting to the lee.
Through the smother and the rout
The *Calliope* steamed out—
And they cheered her from the *Trenton* that was foundering in the sea.

Ay! drifting shoreward there,
All helpless as they were,
Their vessel hurled upon the reefs as weed ashore is hurled,
Without a thought of fear
The Yankees raised a cheer—
A cheer that English-speaking folk should echo round the world.

DO
THEY KNOW?

Do they know? At the turn to the straight
  Where the favourites fail,
And every last atom of weight
  Is telling its tale;
As some grim old stayer hard-pressed
  Runs true to his breed,
And with head just in front of the rest
  Fights on in the lead;
When the jockeys are out with the whips,
  With a furlong to go,
And the backers grow white to the lips—
  Do you think *they* don't know?

Do they know? As they come back to weigh
  In a whirlwind of cheers,
Though the spurs have left marks of the fray
  Though the sweat on the ears
Gathers cold, and they sob with distress
  As they roll up the track,
They know just as well their success
  As the man on their back.
As they walk through a dense human lane
  That sways to and fro,
And cheers them again and again,
  Do you think *they* don't know?

PASSING
OF GUNDAGAI

"I'll introdooce a friend!" he said,
  "And if you've got a vacant pen
You'd better take him in the shed
And start him shearing straight ahead;
  He's one of these here quiet men.

"He never strikes—that ain't his game;
  No matter what the others try
He goes on shearing just the same.
I never rightly knew his name—
  We always call him 'Gundagai!'"

Our flashest shearer then had gone
  To train a racehorse for a race;
And, while his sporting fit was on
He couldn't be relied upon,
  So Gundagai shore in his place.

Alas for man's veracity!
  For reputations false and true!
This Gundagai turned out to be
For strife and all-round villainy
  The very worst I ever knew!

He started racing Jack Devine,
  And grumbled when I made him stop.
The pace he showed was extra fine,
But all those pure-bred ewes of mine
  Were bleeding like a butcher's shop.

He cursed the sheep, he cursed the shed,
  From roof to rafter, floor to shelf:
As for my mongrel ewes, he said,
I ought to get a razor-blade
  And shave the blooming things myself.

On Sundays he controlled a "school",
  And played "two-up" the livelong day;
And many a young confiding fool
He shore of his financial wool;
  And when he lost he would not pay.

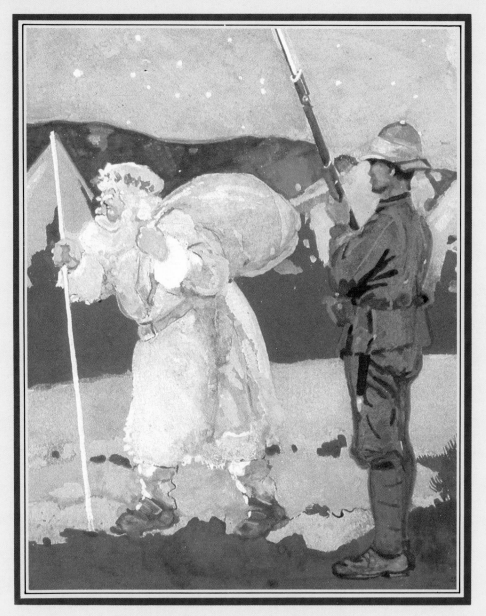

''Halt! Who goes there?'', from *Santa Claus,*
the final poem in *Rio Grande*—the title page vignette
prepared by Gye for this volume

He organised a shearers' race,
    And "touched" me to provide the prize.
His pack-horse showed surprising pace
And won hands down—he was The Ace,
    A well-known racehorse in disguise.

Next day the bruiser of the shed
    Displayed an opal-tinted eye,
With large contusions on his head,
He smiled a sickly smile, and said
    He'd "had a cut at Gundagai!"

But, just as we were getting full
    Of Gundagai and all his ways,
A telegram for "Henry Bull"
Arrived. Said he, "That's me—all wool!
    Let's see what this here message says."

He opened it; his face grew white,
    He dropped the shears and turned away
It ran, "Your wife took bad last night;
Come home at once—no time to write,
    We fear she may not last the day."

He got his cheque—I didn't care
    To dock him for my mangled ewes;
His store account, we called it square,
Poor wretch! he had enough to bear,
    Confronted by such dreadful news.

The shearers raised a little purse
    To help a mate, as shearers will,
"To pay the doctor and the nurse.
And, if there should be something worse,
    To pay the undertaker's bill."

They wrung his hand in sympathy,
    He rode away without a word,
His head hung down in misery . . .
A wandering hawker passing by
    Was told of what had just occurred.

"Well! that's a curious thing," he said,
  "I've known that feller all his life—
He's had the loan of this here shed!
I know his wife ain't nearly dead,
  Because he *hasn't got a wife!*"

        .   .   .   .   .   .

You should have heard the whipcord crack
  As angry shearers galloped by;
In vain they tried to fetch him back—
A little dust along the track
  Was all they saw of "Gundagai".

THE
WARGEILAH HANDICAP

WARGEILAH town is very small,
    There's no cathedral nor a club,
In fact the township, all in all,
    Is just one unpretentious pub;
And there, from all the stations round,
The local sportsmen can be found.

The sportsmen of Wargeilah-side
    Are very few but very fit:
There's scarcely any sport been tried
    But they can hold their own at it;
In fact, to search their records o'er,
They hold their own and something more.

The precincts of Wargeilah town
    An English new-chum did infest:
He used to wander up and down
    In baggy English breeches drest;
His mental aspect seemed to be
Just stolid self-sufficiency.

The local sportsmen vainly sought
    His tranquil calm to counteract
By urging that he should be brought
    Within the Noxious Creatures Act.
"Nay, harm him not," said one more wise,
"He is a blessing in disguise!

"You see, he wants to buy a horse,
    To ride, and hunt, and steeplechase,
And carry ladies, too, of course,
    And pull a cart, and win a race.
Good gracious! he must be a flat
To think he'll get a horse like that!

"But, since he has so little sense
    And such a lot of cash to burn,
We'll sell him some experience
    By which alone a fool can learn.
Suppose we let him have The Trap
To win Wargeilah Handicap!"

163

And here, I must explain to you
   That round about Wargeilah run
There lived a very aged screw
   Whose days of brilliancy were done.
A grand old warrior in his prime—
But age will beat us all in time.

A trooper's horse in seasons past
   He did his share to keep the peace,
But took to falling, and at last
   Was cast for age from the Police.
A publican at Conroy's Gap
Bought him and christened him The Trap.

When grass was good and horses dear,
   He changed his owner now and then
At prices ranging somewhere near
   The neighbourhood of two-pound-ten:
And manfully he earned his keep
By yarding cows and ration sheep.

They brought him in from off the grass
   And fed and groomed the old horse up;
His coat began to shine like glass—
   You'd think he'd win the Melbourne Cup.
And when they'd got him fat and flash
They asked the new-chum—fifty—cash!

And when he said the price was high,
   Their indignation knew no bounds.
They said, "It's seldom you can buy
   A horse like that for fifty pounds!
We'll refund twenty if The Trap
Should fail to win the handicap!"

The deed was done, the price was paid,
   The new-chum put the horse in train.
The local sports were much afraid
   That he would sad experience gain
By racing with some shearer's hack,
Who'd beat him half-way round the track.

So, on this guileless English spark
  They did most fervently impress
That he must keep the matter dark,
  And not let any person guess
That he was purchasing The Trap
To win Wargeilah Handicap.

They spoke of "spielers from the Bland",
  And "champions from the Castlereagh",
And gave the youth to understand
  That all of these would stop away,
And spoil the race, if they should hear
That they had got The Trap to fear.

"Keep dark! They'll muster thick as flies
  When once the news gets sent around
We're giving such a splendid prize—
  A Snowdon horse worth fifty pound!
They'll come right in from Dandaloo,
And find—that it's a gift to you!"

The race came on—with no display,
  Nor any calling of the card,
But round about the pub all day
  A crowd of shearers, drinking hard,
And using language in a strain
'Twere flattery to call profane.

Our hero, dressed in silk attire—
  Blue jacket and scarlet cap—
With boots that shone like flames of fire,
  Now did his canter on The Trap,
And walked him up and round about,
Until the other steeds came out.

He eyed them with a haughty look,
  But saw a sight that caught his breath!
It was Ah John! the Chinee cook!
  In boots and breeches! pale as death!
Tied with a rope, like any sack,
Upon a piebald pony's back!

The next, a colt—all mud and burrs,
　　Half-broken, with a black boy up,
Who said, "You gim'me pair o' spurs,
　　I win the bloomin' Melbourne Cup!"
These two were to oppose The Trap
For the Wargeilah Handicap!

They're off! The colt whipped down his head,
　　And humped his back, and gave a squeal,
And bucked into the drinking shed,
　　Revolving like a Catherine wheel!
Men ran like rats! The atmosphere
Was filled with oaths and pints of beer!

But up the course the bold Ah John
　　Beside The Trap raced neck and neck:
The boys had tied him firmly on,
　　Which ultimately proved his wreck;
The saddle turned, and, like a clown,
He rode some distance upside-down.

His legs around the horse were tied,
　　His feet towards the heavens were spread,
He swung and bumped at every stride
　　And ploughed the ground up with his head!
And when they rescued him, The Trap
Had won Wargeilah Handicap!

And no enquiries we could make
　　Could tell by what false statements swayed
Ah John was led to undertake
　　A task so foreign to his trade!
He only smiled and said, "Hoo Ki!
I stop topside, I win all li'!"

But never in Wargeilah Town
　　Was heard so eloquent a cheer
As when the President came down,
　　And toasted, in Colonial beer,
"The finest rider on the course!
The winner of the Snowdon Horse!

"You go and get your prize," he said;
  "He's with a wild mob, somewhere round
The mountains near the Watershed;
  He's honestly worth fifty pound—
A noble horse, indeed, to win,
But none of *us* can run him in!

"We've chased him poor, we've chased him fat,
  We've run him till our horses dropped;
But by such obstacles as that
  A man like you will not be stopped;
You'll go and yard him any day,
So here's your health! Hooray! Hooray!"

.   .   .   .   .   .

The day wound up with booze and blow
  And fights till all were well content.
But of the new-chum all I know
  Is shown by this advertisement—
"For Sale, the well-known racehorse Trap.
He won Wargeilah Handicap!"

ANY OTHER TIME

ALL of us play our very best game—
  Any other time.
Golf or billiards, it's all the same—
  Any other time.
Lose a match and you always say,
"Just my luck! I was 'off' today!
I could have beaten him quite half-way—
  Any other time!"

After a fiver you ought to go—
  Any other time.
Every man that you ask says "Oh,
  Any *other* time.
Lend you a fiver? I'd lend you two,
But I'm overdrawn and my bills are due,
Wish you'd ask me—now, mind you do—
  Any other time!"

Fellows will ask you out to dine—
  Any other time.
"Not tonight for we're twenty-nine—
  Any other time.
Not tomorrow, for cook's on strike;
Not next day, I'll be out on the bike;
Just drop in whenever you like
  Any other time!"

Seasick passengers like the sea—
  Any other time.
"Something . . I ate . . disagreed . . with . . me!
  Any other time.
Ocean-travelling is . . simply bliss,
Must be my . . liver . . has gone amiss . .
Why, I would . . laugh . . at a sea . . like this—
  Any other time!"

Most of us mean to be better men—
  Any other time:
Regular upright characters then—
  Any other time.
Yet somehow as the years go by
Still we gamble and drink and lie,
When it comes to the last we'll want to die—
  Any other time!

THE
LAST TRUMP

"You led the trump," the old man said
  With fury in his eye,
"And yet you hope my girl to wed!
Young man! your hopes of love are fled,
  'Twere better she should die!

"My sweet young daughter sitting there,
  So innocent and plump!
You don't suppose that she would care
To wed an outlawed man who'd dare
  To lead the thirteenth trump!

"If you had drawn their leading spade
  It meant a certain win!
But no! By Pembroke's mighty shade
The thirteenth trump you went and played
  And let their diamonds in!

"My girl, return at my command
  His presents in a lump!
Return his ring! For, understand,
No man is fit to hold your hand
  Who leads a thirteenth trump!

"But hold! Give every man his due
  And every dog his day.
Speak up and say what made you do
This dreadful thing—that is, if you
  Have anything to say!"

He spoke. "I meant at first," said he,
  "To give their spades a bump,
Or lead the hearts; but then you see
I thought against us there might be,
  Perhaps, a fourteenth trump!"

   .   .   .   .

They buried him at dawn of day
  Beside a ruined stump:
And there he sleeps the hours away
And waits for Gabriel to play
  The last—the fourteenth trump.

TAR
AND FEATHERS

OH! the circus swooped down
On the Narrabri town,
For the Narrabri populace moneyed are;
And the showman he smiled
At the folk he beguiled
To come all the distance from Gunnedah.

But a juvenile smart,
Who objected to "part",
Went in on the nod, and to do it he
Crawled in through a crack
In the tent at the back,
For the boy had no slight ingenuity.

And says he with a grin,
"That's the way to get in;
But I reckon I'd better be quiet or
They'll spiflicate me,"
And he chuckled, for he
Had the loan of the circus proprietor.

But the showman astute
On that wily galoot
Soon dropped—you'll be thinking he leathered
him—
Not he; with a grim
Sort of humorous whim,
He took him and tarred him and feathered him.

Says he, "You can go
Round the world with a show,
And knock every Injun and Arab wry;
With your name and your trade
On the posters displayed,
The feathered what-is-it from Narrabri."

Next day for his freak
By a Narrabri Beak,
He was jawed with a deal of verbosity;
For his only appeal
Was "professional zeal"—
He wanted another monstrosity.

Said his Worship, "Begob!
You are fined forty bob,
And six shillin's costs to the clurk!" he says.
And the Narrabri joy,
Half bird and half boy,
Has a "down" on himself and on circuses.

IT'S GRAND

It's grand to be a squatter
  And sit upon a post,
And watch your little ewes and lambs
  A-giving up the ghost.

It's grand to be a "cockie"
  With wife and kids to keep,
And find an all-wise Providence
  Has mustered all your sheep.

It's grand to be a Western man,
  With a shovel in your hand,
To dig your little homestead out
  From underneath the sand.

It's grand to be a shearer
  Along the Darling-side,
And pluck the wool from stinking sheep
  That some days since have died.

It's grand to be a rabbit
  And breed till all is blue,
And then to die in heaps because
  There's nothing left to chew.

It's grand to be a Minister
  And travel like a swell,
And tell the Central District folk
  To go to—Inverell.

It's grand to be a socialist
  And lead the bold array
That marches to prosperity
  At seven bob a day.

It's grand to be an unemployed
  And lie in the Domain,
And wake up every second day—
  And go to sleep again.

It's grand to borrow English tin
    To pay for wharves and docks
And then to find it isn't in
    The little money-box.

It's grand to be a democrat
    And toady to the mob,
For fear that if you told the truth
    They'd hunt you from your job.

It's grand to be a lot of things
    In this fair Southern land,
But if the Lord would send us rain,
    That would, indeed, be grand!

OUT OF SIGHT

THEY held a polo meeting at a little country town,
And all the local sportsmen came to win themselves renown.
There came two strangers with a horse, and I am much afraid
They both belonged to what is called "the take-you-down brigade".

They said their horse could jump like fun, and asked an amateur
To ride him in the steeplechase, and told him they were sure
The last time round he'd sail away with such a swallow's flight
The rest would never see him go—he'd finish out of sight.

So out he went; and, when folk saw the amateur was up,
Some local genius called the race "the Dude-in-Danger Cup".
The horse was known as "Who's Afraid", by "Panic" from "The
        Fright"—
But still his owners told the jock he'd finish out of sight.

And so he did; for Who's Afraid, without the least pretence,
Disposed of him by rushing through the very second fence;
And when they ran the last time round the prophecy was right—
For he was in the ambulance, and safely "out of sight".

THE ROAD
TO OLD MAN'S TOWN

THE fields of youth are filled with flowers,
The wine of youth is strong:
What need have we to count the hours?
The summer days are long.

But soon we find to our dismay
That we are drifting down
The barren slopes that fall away
Towards the foothills grim and grey
That lead to Old Man's Town.

And marching with us on the track
Full many friends we find:
We see them looking sadly back
For those who've dropped behind.

But God forfend a fate so dread—
Alone to travel down
The dreary road we all must tread,
With faltering steps and whitening head,
The road to Old Man's Town!

THE OLD TIMER'S
STEEPLECHASE

THE sheep were shorn and the wool went down
   At the time of our local racing;
And I'd earned a spell—I was burnt and brown—
So I rolled my swag for a trip to town
   And a look at the steeplechasing.

'Twas rough and ready—an uncleared course
   As rough as the blacks had found it;
With barbed-wire fences, topped with gorse,
And a water-jump that would drown a horse,
   And the steeple three times round it.

There was never a fence the tracks to guard,—
   Some straggling posts defined 'em:
And the day was hot, and the drinking hard,
Till none of the stewards could see a yard
   Before nor yet behind 'em!

But the bell was rung and the nags were out,
   Excepting an old outsider
Whose trainer started an awful rout,
For his boy had gone on a drinking bout
   And left him without a rider.

"Is there not a man in the crowd," he cried,
   "In the whole of the crowd so clever,
Is there not one man that will take a ride
On the old white horse from the Northern side
   That was bred on the Mooki River?"

'Twas an old white horse that they called The Cow,
   And a cow would look well beside him;
But I was pluckier then than now
(And I wanted excitement anyhow),
   So at last I agreed to ride him.

And the trainer said, "Well, he's dreadful slow,
   And he hasn't a chance whatever;
But I'm stony broke, so it's time to show
A trick or two that the trainers know
   Who train by the Mooki River.

"The first time round at the futher side,
  With the trees and the scrub about you,
Just pull behind them and run out wide
And then dodge into the scrub and hide,
  And let them go round without you.

"At the third time round, for the final spin
  With the pace and the dust to blind 'em,
They'll never notice if you chip in
For the last half-mile—you'll be sure to win,
  And they'll think you raced behind 'em.

"At the water-jump you may have to swim—
  He hasn't a hope to clear it,
Unless he skims like the swallows skim
At full speed over—but not for him!
  He'll never go next or near it.

"But don't you worry—just plunge across,
  For he swims like a well-trained setter.
Then hide away in the scrub and gorse
The rest will be far ahead, of course—
  The further ahead the better.

"You must rush the jumps in the last half-round
  For fear that he might refuse 'em;
He'll try to baulk with you, I'll be bound;
Take whip and spurs to the mean old hound,
  And don't be afraid to use 'em.

"At the final round, when the field are slow
  And you are quite fresh to meet 'em,
Sit down, and hustle him all you know
With the whip and spurs, and he'll have to go—
  Remember, you've *got* to beat 'em!"

     .   .   .   .   .   .

The flag went down, and we seemed to fly,
  And we made the timbers shiver
Of the first big fence, as the stand flashed by,
And I caught the ring of the trainer's cry:
  "Go on, for the Mooki River!"

I jammed him in with a well-packed crush,
  And recklessly—out for slaughter—
Like a living wave over fence and brush
We swept and swung with a flying rush,
  Till we came to the dreaded water.

Ha, ha! I laugh at it now to think
  Of the way I contrived to work it.
Shut in amongst them, before you'd wink,
He found himself on the water's brink,
  With never a chance to shirk it!

The thought of the horror he felt beguiles
  The heart of this grizzled rover!
He gave a snort you could hear for miles,
And a spring would have cleared the Channel Isles,
  And carried me safely over!

Then we neared the scrub, and I pulled him back
  In the shade where the gum-leaves quiver:
And I waited there in the shadows black
While the rest of the horses, round the track,
  Went on like a rushing river!

At the second round, as the field swept by,
  I saw that the pace was telling;
But on they thundered, and by-and-by
As they passed the stand I could hear the cry
  Of the folk in the distance, yelling!

Then the last time round! And the hoofbeats rang!
  And I said, "Well, it's now or never!"
And out on the heels of the throng I sprang,
And the spurs bit deep and the whipcord sang
  As I rode. For the Mooki River!

We raced for home in a cloud of dust
  And the curses rose in chorus.
'Twas flog, and hustle, and jump you must!
And The Cow ran well—but to my disgust
  There was one got home before us.

'Twas a big black horse, that I had not seen
  In the part of the race I'd ridden;
And his coat was cool and his rider clean—
And I thought that perhaps I had not been
  The only one that had hidden.

And the trainer came with a visage blue
  With rage, when the race concluded:
Said he, "I thought you'd have pulled us through,
But the man on the black horse planted too,
  And nearer to home than you did!"

     ·   ·   ·   ·   ·   ·

Alas to think that those times so gay
  Have vanished and passed for ever!
You don't believe in the yarn, you say?
Why, man, 'twas a matter of every day
  When we raced on the Mooki River!

IN
THE STABLE

WHAT! you don't like him; well, maybe—we all have our fancies,
    of course:
Brumby to look at, you reckon? Well, no; he's a thoroughbred horse;
Sired by a son of old Panic—look at his ears and his head—
Lop-eared and Roman-nosed, ain't he?—well, that's how the Panics
    are bred.
Gluttonous, ugly and lazy, rough as a tip-cart to ride,
Yet if you offered a sovereign apiece for the hairs on his hide
That wouldn't buy him, nor twice that; while I've a pound to
    the good,
This here old stager stays by me and lives like a thoroughbred
    should;
Hunt him away from his bedding, and sit yourself down by the wall,
Till you hear how the old fellow saved me from Gilbert, O'Meally
    and Hall.

.   .   .   .   .   .

Gilbert and Hall and O'Meally, back in the bushranging days,
Made themselves kings of the district—ruled it in old-fashioned
    ways—
Robbing the coach and the escort, stealing our horses at night,
Calling sometimes at the homesteads and giving the women a fright:
Came to the station one morning (and why they did this no one
    knows)
Took a brood mare from the paddock—wanting some fun, I
    suppose—
Fastened a bucket beneath her, hung by a strap around her flank,
Then turned her loose in the timber back of the seven-mile tank.

Go? She went mad! She went tearing and screaming with fear
    through the trees,
While the curst bucket beneath her was banging her flanks and
    her knees.
Bucking and racing and screaming she ran to the back of the run,
Killed herself there in a gully; by God, but they paid for their fun!
Paid for it dear, for the black-boys found tracks, and the bucket,
    and all,
And I swore that I'd live to get even with Gilbert, O'Meally and
    Hall.

Day after day then I chased them—'course they had friends on
the sly,
Friends who were willing to sell them to those who were willing
to buy.
Early one morning we found them in camp at the Cockatoo Farm;
One of us shot at O'Meally and wounded him under the arm:
Ran them for miles in the ranges, till Hall, with his horse fairly
beat,
Took to the rocks and we lost him—the others made good their
retreat.

It was war to the knife then, I tell you, and once, on the door of my
shed,
They nailed up a notice that offered a hundred reward for my head!
Then we heard they were gone from the district; they stuck up
a coach in the West,
And I rode by myself in the paddocks, just taking a bit of a rest,
Riding this colt as a youngster—awkward, half-broken and shy,
He wheeled round one day on a sudden; I looked, but I couldn't
see why—
But I soon found out why, for before me the hillside rose up like
a wall,
And there on the top with their rifles were Gilbert, O'Meally
and Hall!

'Twas a good three-mile run to the homestead—bad going, with
plenty of trees—
So I gathered the youngster together, and gripped at his ribs with
my knees.
'Twas a mighty poor chance to escape them! It puts a man's
nerve to the test
On a half-broken colt to be hunted by the best mounted men in
the West.
But the half-broken colt was a racehorse! He lay down to work
with a will.
Flashed through the scrub like a clean-skin—by heavens, we *flew*
down the hill!
Over a twenty-foot gully he swept with the spring of a deer,
And they fired as we jumped, but they missed me—a bullet sang
close to my ear—
And the jump gained us ground, for they shirked it: but I **saw**
as we raced through the gap

That the rails at the homestead were fastened—I was caught like
   a rat in a trap.
Fenced with barbed wire was the paddock—barbed wire that would
   cut like a knife—
How was a youngster to clear it that never had jumped in his life?

Bang went a rifle behind me—the colt gave a spring, he was hit;
Straight at the sliprails I rode him—I felt him take hold of the bit;
Never a foot to the right or the left did he swerve in his stride,
Awkward and frightened, but honest, the sort it's a pleasure to ride!
Straight at the rails, where they'd fastened barbed wire on the top
   of the post,
Rose like a stag and went over, with hardly a scratch at the most;
Into the homestead I darted, and snatched down my gun from
   the wall,
And I tell you I made them step lively, Gilbert, O'Meally and Hall.

Yes! There's the mark of the bullet—he's got it inside of him yet,
Mixed up somehow with his victuals; but, bless you, he don't seem
   to fret!
Gluttonous, ugly, and lazy—eats anything he can bite;
Now, let us shut up the stable, and bid the old fellow good night.
Ah! we can't breed 'em, the sort that were bred when we old uns
   were young. . . .
Yes, as I said, these bushrangers, none of 'em lived to be hung.
Gilbert was shot by the troopers, Hall was betrayed by his friend,
Campbell disposed of O'Meally, bringing the lot to an end.
But you can talk about riding—I've ridden a lot in the past—
Wait till there's rifles behind you, you'll know what it means to
   go fast!
I've steeplechased, raced, and "run horses", but I think the most
   dashing of all
Was the ride when that old fellow saved me from Gilbert, O'Meally
   and Hall!

"HE GIVETH
HIS BELOVED SLEEP"

THE long day passes with its load of sorrow:
   In slumber deep
I lay me down to rest until tomorrow—
   Thank God for sleep.

Thank God for all respite from weary toiling,
   From cares that creep
Across our lives like evil shadows, spoiling
   God's kindly sleep.

We plough and sow, and, as the hours grow later,
   We strive to reap,
And build our barns, and hope to build them greater
   Before we sleep.

We toil and strain and strive with one another
   In hopes to heap
Some greater share of profit than our brother
   Before we sleep.

What will it profit that with tears or laughter
   Our watch we keep?
Beyond it all there lies the Great Hereafter!
   Thank God for sleep!

For, at the last, beseeching Christ to save us,
   We turn with deep
Heart-felt thanksgiving unto God, who gave us
   The Gift of Sleep.

DRIVER
SMITH

'Twas Driver Smith of Battery A was anxious to see a fight;
He thought of the Transvaal all the day, he thought of it all the
       night—
"Well, if the battery's left behind, I'll go to the war," says he,
"I'll go a-driving an ambulance in the ranks of the A.M.C.

"I'm fairly sick of these here parades—it's want of a change that
       kills—
A-charging the Randwick Rifle Range and aiming at Surry Hills.
And I think if I go with the ambulance I'm certain to find a show,
For they have to send the Medical men wherever the troops can go.

"Wherever the rifle bullets flash and the Maxims raise a din,
It's here you'll find the Medical men a-raking the wounded in—
A-raking 'em in like human flies—and a driver smart like me
Will find some scope for his extra skill in the ranks of the A.M.C."

So Driver Smith he went to the war a-cracking his driver's whip,
From ambulance to collecting base they showed him his regular trip.
And he said to the boys that were marching past, as he gave his
      whip a crack,
"You'll walk yourselves to the fight," says he—"Lord spare me, I'll
      drive you back."

Now, the fight went on in the Transvaal hills for the half of a day
      or more,
And Driver Smith he worked his trip—all aboard for the seat of war!
He took his load from the stretcher men and hurried 'em homeward
      fast
Till he heard a sound that he knew full well—a battery rolling
      past.

He heard the clink of the leading chains and the roll of the guns
      behind—
He heard the crack of the drivers' whips, and he says to 'em,
      "Strike me blind,
I'll miss me trip with this ambulance, although I don't care to
      shirk,
But I'll take the car off the line today and follow the guns at work."

Then up the Battery Colonel came a-cursing 'em black in the face.
"Sit down and shift 'em, you drivers there, and gallop 'em into
    place."
So off the Battery rolled and swung, a-going a merry dance,
And holding his own with the leading gun goes Smith with his
    ambulance.

They opened fire on the mountain side, a-peppering by and large,
When over the hill above their flank the Boers came down at the
    charge;
They rushed the guns with a daring rush, a-volleying left and right,
And Driver Smith and his ambulance moved up to the edge of
    the fight.

The gunners stuck to their guns like men, and fought as the wild
    cats fight,
For a Battery man don't leave his gun with ever a hope in sight;
But the bullets sang and the Mausers cracked and the Battery
    men gave way,
Till Driver Smith with his ambulance drove into the thick of
    the fray.

He saw the head of the Transvaal troop a-thundering to and fro,
A hard old face with a monkey beard—a face that he seemed
    to know;
"Now, who's that leader?" said Driver Smith. "I've seen him before
    today.
Why, bless my heart, but it's Kruger's self," and he jumped for him
    straight away.

He collared old Kruger round the waist and hustled him into the
    van.
It wasn't according to stretcher drill for raising a wounded man;
But he forced him in and said, "All aboard, we're off for a little ride,
And you'll have the car to yourself," says he, "I reckon we're full
    inside."

He wheeled his team on the mountain side and set 'em a merry pace,
A-galloping over the rocks and stones, and a lot of the Boers gave
    chase;
But Driver Smith had a fairish start, and he said to the Boers,
    "Good-day,
You have Buckley's chance for to catch a man that was trained
    in Battery A."

He drove his team to the hospital and said to the P.M.O.,
"Beg pardon, sir, but I missed a trip, mistaking the way to go;
And Kruger came to the ambulance and asked could we spare a bed,
So I fetched him here, and we'll take him home to show for a
      bob a head."

So the word went round to the English troops to say they need
      fight no more,
For Driver Smith with his ambulance had ended the blooming war.
And in London now at the music halls he's starring it every night,
And drawing a hundred pounds a week to tell how he won the fight.

THERE'S ANOTHER
BLESSED HORSE FELL DOWN

WHEN you're lying in your hammock, sleeping soft and sleeping
  sound,
 Without a care or trouble on your mind,
And there's nothing to disturb you but the engines going round,
 And you're dreaming of the girl you left behind;
In the middle of your joys you'll be wakened by a noise
 And a clatter on the deck above your crown,
And you'll hear the corporal shout as he turns the picket out,
 "There's another blessed horse fell down."

You can see 'em in the morning, when you're cleaning out the stall,
 A-leaning on the railings nearly dead,
And you reckon by the evening they'll be pretty sure to fall,
 And you curse them as you tumble into bed.
Oh, you'll hear it pretty soon, "Pass the word for Denny Moon,
 There's a horse here throwing handsprings like a clown;"
And it's shove the others back, or he'll cripple half the pack;
 "There's another blessed horse fell down."

And when the war is over and the fighting all is done,
 And you're all at home with medals on your chest,
And you've learnt to sleep so soundly that the firing of a gun
 At your bedside wouldn't rob you of your rest;
As you lay in slumber deep, if your wife walks in her sleep,
 And tumbles down the stairs and breaks her crown,
Oh, it won't awaken you, for you'll say, "It's nothing new,
 It's another blessed horse fell down."

ON
THE TREK

OH, the weary, weary journey on the trek, day after day,
  With sun above and silent veldt below;
And our hearts keep turning homeward to the youngsters far away,
  And the homestead where the climbing roses grow.
Shall we see the flats grow golden with the ripening of the grain?
  Shall we hear the parrots calling on the bough?
Ah! the weary months of marching ere we hear them call again,
  For we're going on a long job now.

In the drowsy days on escort, riding slowly half asleep,
  With the endless line of waggons stretching back,
While the khaki soldiers travel like a mob of travelling sheep,
  Plodding silent on the never-ending track,
While the constant snap and sniping of the foe you never see
  Makes you wonder will your turn come—when and how?
As the Mauser ball hums past you like a vicious kind of bee—
  Oh! we're going on a long job now.

When the dash and the excitement and the novelty are dead,
  And you've seen a load of wounded once or twice,
Or you've watched your old mate dying, with the vultures over-
        head—
  Well, you wonder if the war is worth the price.
And down along the Monaro now they're starting out to shear,
  I can picture the excitement and the row;
But they'll miss me on the Lachlan when they call the roll this year,
  For we're going on a long job now.

THE
LAST PARADE

WITH never a sound of trumpet,
  With never a flag displayed,
The last of the old campaigners
  Lined up for the last parade.

Weary they were and battered,
  Shoeless, and knocked about;
From under their ragged forelocks
  Their hungry eyes looked out.

And they watched as the old commander
  Read out to the cheering men
The Nation's thanks, and the orders
  To carry them home again.

And the last of the old campaigners,
  Sinewy, lean, and spare—
He spoke for his hungry comrades:
  "Have we not done our share?

"Starving and tired and thirsty
  We limped on the blazing plain;
And after a long night's picket
  You saddled us up again.

"We froze on the wind-swept kopjes
  When the frost lay snowy-white,
Never a halt in the daytime,
  Never a rest at night!

"We knew when the rifles rattled
  From the hillside bare and brown,
And over our weary shoulders
  We felt warm blood run down,

"As we turned for the stretching gallop,
  Crushed to the earth with weight;
But we carried our riders through it—
  Sometimes, perhaps, too late.

"Steel! We were steel to stand it—
  We that have lasted through,
We that are old campaigners
  Pitiful, poor, and few.

"Over the sea you brought us,
  Over the leagues of foam:
Now we have served you fairly
  Will you not take us home?

"Home to the Hunter River,
  To the flats where the lucerne grows;
Home where the Murrumbidgee
  Runs white with the melted snows.

"This is a small thing, surely!
  Will not you give command
That the last of the old campaigners
  Go back to their native land?"

.   .   .   .   .   .

They looked at the grim commander,
  But never a sign he made.
"Dismiss!" and the old campaigners
  Moved off from their last parade.

JOHNNY
BOER

MEN fight all shapes and sizes as the racing horses run,
And no man knows his courage till he stands before a gun.
At mixed-up fighting, hand to hand, and clawing men about
They reckon Fuzzy-Wuzzy is the hottest fighter out.
But Fuzzy gives himself away—his style is out of date,
He charges like a driven grouse that rushes on its fate;
You've nothing in the world to do but pump him full of lead:
But when you're fighting Johnny Boer you have to use your head;
He don't believe in front attacks or charging at the run,
He fights you from a kopje with his little Maxim gun.

For when the Lord He made the earth, it seems uncommon clear,
He gave the job of Africa to some good engineer,
Who started building fortresses on fashions of his own—
Lunettes, redoubts, and counterscarps all made of rock and stone.
The Boer need only bring a gun, for ready to his hand
He finds these heaven-built fortresses all scattered through the land;
And there he sits and winks his eye and wheels his gun about,
And we must charge across the plain to hunt the beggar out.
It ain't a game that grows on us—there's lots of better fun
Than charging at old Johnny with his little Maxim gun.

On rocks a goat could scarcely climb, steep as the walls of Troy,
He wheels a four-point-seven about as easy as a toy;
With bullocks yoked and drag-ropes manned, he lifts her up the
        rocks.
And shifts her every now and then, as cunning as a fox.
At night you mark her right ahead, you see her clean and clear,
Next day at dawn—"What, ho! she bumps"—from somewhere in
        the rear.
Or else the keenest-eyed patrol will miss him with the glass—
He's lying hidden in the rocks to let the leaders pass;
But when the mainguard comes along he opens up the fun;
There's lots of ammunition for the little Maxim gun.

But after all the job is sure, although the job is slow.
We have to see the business through, the Boer has got to go.
With Nordenfeldt and lyddite shell it's certain, soon or late,
We'll hunt him from his kopjes and across the Orange State;
And then across those open flats you'll see the beggar run,
And we'll be running after him with *our* little Maxim gun.

RIGHT IN FRONT OF THE ARMY

"WHERE 'ave you been this week or more,
'Aven't seen you about the war?
Thought perhaps you was at the rear
Guarding the waggons." "What, us? No fear!
Where have we been? Why, bless my heart,
Where have we been since the bloomin' start?
    Right in the front of the army,
      Battling day and night!
    Right in the front of the army
      Teaching 'em how to fight!"
    Every separate man you see,
    Sapper, gunner, and C.I.V.,
    Every one of 'em seems to be
    Right in front of the army!

Most of the troops to the camp had gone,
When we met with a cow-gun toiling on;
And we said to the boys, as they walked her past,
"Well, thank goodness, you're here at last!"
"Here at last! Why, what d'yer mean?
Ain't we just where we've always been?
    Right in the front of the army,
      Battling day and night!
    Right in the front of the army,
      Teaching 'em bow to fight!"
    Correspondents and Vets in force,
    Mounted foot and dismounted horse,
    All of them were, as a matter of course,
    Right in the front of the army.

Old Lord Roberts will have to mind
If ever the enemy get behind;
For they'll smash him up with a rear attack,
Because his army has got no back!
Think of the horrors that might befall
An army without any rear at all!

Right in the front of the army,
  Battling day and night!
Right in the front of the army,
  Teaching 'em how to fight!
Swede attaches and German counts,
Yeomen (known as De Wet's Remounts),
All of them were, by their own accounts,
Right in the front of the army!

THAT V.C.

'TWAS in the days of front attack;
  This glorious truth we'd yet to learn it—
That every "front" has got a back.
  And French was just the man to turn it.

A wounded soldier on the ground
  Was lying hid behind a hummock;
He proved the good old proverb sound—
  An army travels on its stomach.

He lay as flat as any fish;
  His nose had worn a little furrow;
He only had one frantic wish,
  That like an ant-bear he could burrow.

The bullets whistled into space,
  The pom-pom gun kept up its braying,
The four-point-seven supplied the bass—
  You'd think the devil's band was playing.

A valiant comrade crawling near
  Observed his most supine behaviour,
And crept towards him; "Hey! what cheer?
  Buck up," said he, "I've come to save yer.

"You get up on my shoulders, mate,
  And, if we live beyond the firing,
I'll get the V.C. sure as fate,
  Because our blokes is all retiring.

"It's fifty pound a year," says he,
  "I'll stand you lots of beer and whisky."
"No," says the wounded man, "not me,
  I'll not be saved—it's far too risky.

"I'm fairly safe behind this mound,
  I've worn a hole that seems to fit me;
But if you lift me off the ground
  It's fifty pounds to one they'll hit me."

So back towards the firing-line
   Our friend crept slowly to the rear-oh!
Remarking "What a selfish swine!
   He might have let me be a hero."

JOCK

THERE'S a soldier that's been doing of his share
  In the fighting up and down and round about.
He's continually marching here and there,
  And he's fighting, morning in and morning out.
The Boer, you see, he generally runs;
  But sometimes, when he hides behind a rock,
And we can't make no impression with the guns,
  Oh, then you'll hear the order, "Send for Jock!"

  Yes—it's Jock—Scotch Jock.
  He's the fellow that can give or take a knock.
  For he's hairy and he's hard,
  And his feet are by the yard,
  And his face is like the face what's on a clock.
  But when the bullets fly you will mostly hear the cry—
  "Send for Jock!"

The Cavalry have gun and sword and lance;
  Before they choose their weapon, why, they're dead.
The Mounted Foot are hampered in advance
  By holding of their helmets on their head.
And, when the Boer has dug himself a trench
  And placed his Maxim gun behind a rock,
These mounted heroes—pets of Johnny French—
  They have to sit and wait and send for Jock!

  Yes, the Jocks—Scotch Jocks,
  With their music that'd terrify an ox!
  When the bullets kick the sand
  You can hear the sharp command—
  "Forty-Second! At the double! Charge the rocks!"
  And the charge is like a flood
  When they warmed the Highland blood
  Of the Jocks!

SANTA CLAUS

"HALT! Who goes there?" The sentry's call
Rose on the midnight air
Above the noises of the camp,
The roll of wheels, the horses' tramp.
The challenge echoed over all—
"Halt! Who goes there?"

A quaint old figure clothed in white,
He bore a staff of pine,
An ivy-wreath was on his head.
"Advance, O friend," the sentry said,
"Advance, for this is Christmas Night,
And give the countersign."

"No sign nor countersign have I.
Through many lands I roam
The whole world over far and wide.
To exiles all at Christmastide
From those who love them tenderly
I bring a thought of home.

"From English brook and Scottish burn,
From cold Canadian snows,
From those far lands ye hold most dear
I bring you all a greeting here,
A frond of a New Zealand fern,
A bloom of English rose.

"From faithful wife and loving lass
I bring a wish divine,
For Christmas blessings on your head."
"I wish you well," the sentry said,
"But here, alas! you may not pass
Without the countersign."

He vanished—and the sentry's tramp
Re-echoed down the line.
It was not till the morning light
The soldiers knew that in the night
Old Santa Claus had come to camp
Without the countersign.

III
SALTBUSH BILL, J.P., AND OTHER VERSES

SONG OF
THE WHEAT

We have sung the song of the droving days,
  Of the march of the travelling sheep—
How by silent stages and lonely ways
  Thin, white battalions creep.
But the man who now by the land would thrive
  Must his spurs to a ploughshare beat;
And the bush bard, changing his tune, may strive
  To sing the song of the Wheat!

It's west by south of the Great Divide
  The grim grey plains run out,
Where the old flock-masters lived and died
  In a ceaseless fight with drought.
Weary with waiting and hope deferred
  They were ready to own defeat,
Till at last they heard the master-word—
  And the master-word was Wheat.

Yarran and Myall and Box and Pine—
  'Twas axe and fire for all;
They scarce could tarry to blaze the line
  Or wait for the trees to fall
Ere the team was yoked, and the gates flung wide,
  And the dust of the horses' feet
Rose up like a pillar of smoke to guide
  The wonderful march of Wheat.

Furrow by furrow, and fold by fold,
  The soil is turned on the plain;
Better than silver and better than gold
  Is the surface-mine of the grain.
Better than cattle and better than sheep
  In the fight with drought and heat;
For a streak of stubbornness, wide and deep,
  Lies hid in a grain of Wheat.

When the stock is swept by the hand of fate,
    Deep down on his bed of clay
The brave brown Wheat will die and wait
    For the resurrection day—
Lie hid while the whole world thinks him dead;
    But the Spring-rain, soft and sweet,
Will over the steaming paddocks spread
    The first green flush of the Wheat.

Green and amber and gold it grows
    When the sun sinks late in the West;
And the breeze sweeps over the rippling rows
    Where the quail and the skylark nest.
Mountain or river or shining star,
    There's never a sight can beat—
Away to the sky-line stretching far—
    A sea of the ripening Wheat.

When the burning harvest sun sinks low,
    And shadows stretch on the plain,
The roaring strippers come and go
    Like ships on a sea of grain.
Till the lurching, groaning waggons bear
    Their tale of the load complete.
Of the world's great work he has done his share
    Who has garnered a crop of wheat.

Princes, Potentates, Kings and Czars,
    They travel in regal state,
But old King Wheat has a thousand cars
    For his trip to the water-gate;
And his thousand steamships breast the tide
    And plough through the wind and sleet
To the lands where the teeming millions bide
    That say: "Thank God for Wheat!"

BRUMBY'S RUN

*Brumby is the Aboriginal Word for a wild horse.
At a recent trial a New South Wales Supreme
Court Judge, hearing of Brumby horses, asked:
"Who is Brumby, and where is his Run?"*

Iт lies beyond the Western Pines
  Beneath the sinking sun,
And not a survey mark defines
  The bounds of "Brumby's Run".

On odds and ends of mountain land,
  On tracks of range and rock
Where no one else can make a stand
  Old Brumby rears his stock.

A wild, unhandled lot they are
  Of every shape and breed.
They venture out 'neath moon and star
  Along the flats to feed;

But, when the dawn makes pink the sky
  And steals along the plain,
The Brumby horses turn and fly
  Back to the hills again.

The traveller by the mountain-track
  May hear their hoof-beats pass,
And catch a glimpse of brown and black
  Dim shadows on the grass.

The eager stock-horse pricks his ears,
  And lifts his head on high
In wild excitement, when he hears
  The Brumby mob go by.

Old Brumby asks no price or fee
  O'er all his wide domains:
The man who yards his stock is free
  To keep them for his pains.

So, off to scour the mountain side
   With eager eyes aglow, ·
To strongholds where the wild mobs hide
   The gully-rakers go.

A rush of horses through the trees,
   A red shirt making play;
A sound of stockwhips on the breeze,
   They vanish far away!

·   ·   ·   ·   ·

Ah, me! before our day is done
   We long with bitter pain
To ride once more on Brumby's Run
   And yard his mob again.

SALTBUSH BILL
ON THE PATRIARCHS

Come all you little rouseabouts and climb upon my knee;
Today, you see, is Christmas Day, and so it's up to me
To give you some instruction like—a kind of Christmas tale—
So name your yarn, and off she goes. What, "Jonah and the Whale?"

Well, whales is sheep I've never shore; I've never been to sea,
So all them great Leviathans is mysteries to me;
But there's a tale the Bible tells I fully understand,
About the time the Patriarchs were settling on the land.

Those Patriarchs of olden time, when all is said and done,
They lived the same as far-out men on many a Queensland run—
A lot of roving, droving men who drifted to and fro,
The same we did out Queensland way a score of years ago.

Now Isaac was a squatter man, and Jacob was his son,
And when the boy grew up, you see, he wearied of the run.
You know the way that boys grow up—there's some that stick
        at home;
But any boy that's worth his salt will roll his swag and roam.

So Jacob caught the roving fit and took the drovers' track
To where his uncle had a run, beyond the outer back;
You see they made for out-back runs for room to stretch and grow,
The same we did out Queensland way a score of years ago.

Now, Jacob knew the ways of stock—that's most uncommon clear—
For, when he got to Laban's Run, they made him overseer;
He didn't ask a pound a week, but bargained for his pay
To take the roan and strawberry calves—the same we'd take today.

The duns and blacks and "Goulburn roans" (that's brindles), coarse
        and hard,
He branded them with Laban's brand, in Old Man Laban's yard;
So, when he'd done the station work for close on seven year,
Why, all the choicest stock belonged to Laban's overseer.

It's often so with overseers—I've seen the same thing done
By many a Queensland overseer on many a Queensland run.
But when the mustering time came on old Laban acted straight,
And gave him country of his own outside the boundary gate.

He gave him stock, and offered him his daughter's hand in troth;
And Jacob first he married one, and then he married both;
You see, they weren't particular about a wife or so—
No more were we up Queensland way a score of years ago.

But when the stock were strong and fat with grass and lots of rain,
Then Jacob felt the call to take the homeward track again.
It's strange in every creed and clime, no matter where you roam,
There comes a day when every man would like to make for home.

So off he set with sheep and goats, a mighty moving band,
To battle down the dusty road along the Overland—
It's droving mixed-up mobs like that that makes men cut their
      throats,
I've travelled rams, which Lord forget, but never travelled goats.

But Jacob knew the ways of stock, for (so the story goes)
When battling through the Philistines—selectors, I suppose—
He thought he'd have to fight his way, an awkward sort of job;
So what did Old Man Jacob do? Of course, he split the mob.

He sent the strong stock on ahead to battle out the way;
He couldn't hurry lambing ewes—no more you could today—
And down the road from run to run, his hand 'gainst every hand,
He moved that mighty mob of stock across the Overland.

The thing is made so clear and plain, so solid in and out,
There isn't any room at all for any kind of doubt.
It's just a plain straightforward tale—a tale that lets you know
The way they lived in Palestine three thousand years ago.

It's strange to read it all today, the shifting of the stock;
You'd think you see the caravans that loaf behind the flock,
The little donkeys and the mules, the sheep that slowly spread,
And maybe Dan or Naphthali a-ridin' on ahead.

The long, dry, dusty summer days, the smouldering fires at night;
The stir and bustle of the camp at break of morning light;
The little kids that skipped about, the camels' dead-slow tramp—
I wish I'd done a week or two in Old Man Jacob's camp!

But if I keep the narrer path some day, perhaps, I'll know
How Jacob bred them strawberry calves three thousand years ago.

THE
REVEREND MULLINEUX

I'D reckon his weight as eight-stun-eight,
  And his height at five-foot-two,
With a face as plain as an eight-day clock
And a walk as brisk as a bantam-cock—
  Game as a bantam, too,
Hard and wiry and full of steam,
That's the boss of the English Team,
  Reverend Mullineux!

Makes no row when the game gets rough—
  None of your "Strike me blue!"
"Yous wants smacking across the snout!"
Plays like a gentleman out-and-out—
  Same as he ought to do.
"Kindly remove from off my face!"
That's the way that he states his case,
  Reverend Mullineux.

Kick! He can kick like an army mule—
  Run like a kangaroo!
Hard to get by as a lawyer-plant,
Tackles his man like a bull-dog ant—
  Fetches him over too!
Didn't the public cheer and shout
Watchin' him chuckin' big blokes about,
  Reverend Mullineux!

Scrimmage was packed on his prostrate form,
  Somehow the ball got through—
Who was it tackled our big half-back,
Flinging him down like an empty sack,
  Right on our goal-line too?
Who but the man that we thought was dead,
Down with a score of 'em on his head,
  Reverend Mullineux.

WISDOM OF
HAFIZ

My son, if you go to the races to battle with Ikey and Mo,
Remember, it's seldom the pigeon can pick out the eye of the crow
Remember, they live by the business; remember, my son, and
    go slow.

If ever an owner should tell you, "Back mine"—don't you be such
    a flat.
He knows his own cunning, no doubt—does he know what the
    others are at?
Find out what he's frightened of most, and invest a few dollars
    on that.

Walk not in the track of the trainer, nor hang round the rails at
    his stall.
His wisdom belongs to his patron—shall he give it to one and to all?
When the stable is served he may tell you—and his words are like
    jewels let fall.

Run wide of the tipster who whispers that Borak is sure to be first,
He tells the next mug that he corners a tale with the placings
    reversed;
And, remember, of judges of racing, the jockey's the absolute worst.

When they lay three to one on the field, and the runners are
    twenty-and-two,
Take a pull on yourself; take a pull—it's a mighty big field to
    get through.
Is the club handicapper a fool? If a fool is about, p'raps it's you!

Beware of the critic who tells you the handicap's absolute rot,
For this is chucked in, and that's hopeless, and somebody ought
    to be shot.
How is it he can't make a fortune himself when he knows such a lot?

From tipsters, and jockeys, and trials, and gallops, the glory has gone,
For this is the wisdom of Hafiz that sages have pondered upon,
"The very best tip in the world is to see the commission go on!"

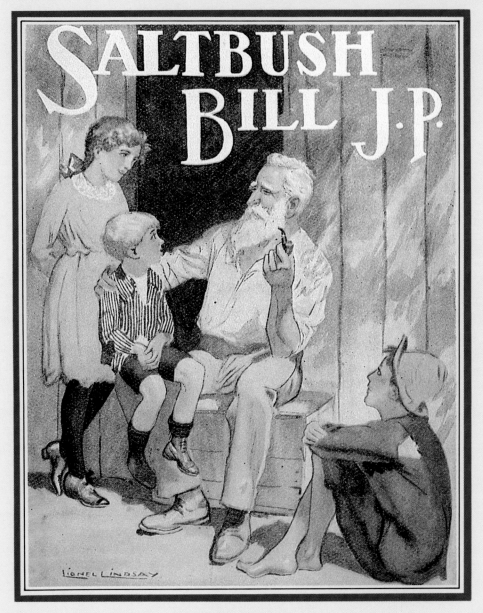

Lionel Lindsay's jacket for
Saltbush Bill, J.P.

SALTBUSH BILL, J.P.

BEYOND the land where Leichhardt went,
  Beyond Sturt's Western track,
The rolling tide of change has sent
  Some strange J.P.'s out back.

And Saltbush Bill, grown old and grey,
  And worn for want of sleep,
Received the news in camp one day
  Behind the travelling sheep.

That Edward Rex, confiding in
  His known integrity,
By hand and seal on parchment skin
  Had made him a J.P.

He read the news with eager face
  But found no word of pay.
"I'd like to see my sister's place
  And kids on Christmas Day.

"I'd like to see green grass again,
  And watch clear water run,
Away from this unholy plain,
  And flies, and dust, and sun."

At last one little clause he found
  That might some hope inspire,
"A magistrate may charge a pound
  For inquest on a fire."

A big blacks' camp was built close by,
  And Saltbush Bill, says he,
"I think that camp might well supply
  A job for a J.P."

That night, by strange coincidence,
  A most disastrous fire
Destroyed the country residence
  Of Jacky Jack, Esquire.

'Twas mostly leaves, and bark, and dirt;
   The party most concerned
Appeared to think it wouldn't hurt
   If forty such were burned.

Quite otherwise thought Saltbush Bill,
   Who watched the leaping flame.
"The home is small," said he, "but still
   The principle's the same.

"Midst palaces though you should roam,
   Or follow pleasure's tracks,
You'll find," he said, "no place like home—
   At least like Jacky Jack's.

"Tell every man in camp, 'Come quick,'
   Tell every black Maria
I give tobacco, half a stick—
   Hold inquest long-a fire."

Each juryman received a name
   Well suited to a Court.
"Long Jack" and "Stumpy Bill" became
   "John Long" and "William Short".

While such as "Tarpot", "Bullock Dray",
   And "Tommy Wait-a-While",
Became, for ever and a day,
   "Scot", "Dickens", and "Carlyle".

And twelve good sable men and true
   Were soon engaged upon
The conflagration that o'erthrew
   The home of John A. John.

Their verdict, "Burnt by act of Fate",
   They scarcely had returned
When, just behind the magistrate,
   Another humpy burned!

The jury sat again and drew
   Another stick of plug.
Said Saltbush Bill, "It's up to you
   Put some one long-a Jug."

"I'll camp the sheep," he said, "and sift
   The evidence about."
For quite a week he couldn't shift,
   The way the fires broke out.

The jury thought the whole concern
   As good as any play.
They used to "take him oath" and earn
   Three sticks of plug a day.

At last the tribe lay down to sleep
   Homeless, beneath a tree;
And onward with his travelling sheep
   Went Saltbush Bill, J.P.

The sheep delivered, safe and sound,
   His horse to town he turned,
And drew some five-and-twenty pound
   For fees that he had earned.

And where Monaro's ranges hide
   Their little farms away—
His sister's children by his side—
   He spent his Christmas Day.

The next J.P. that went out back
   Was shocked, or pained, or both,
At hearing every pagan black
   Repeat the juror's oath.

No matter though he turned and fled
   They followed faster still;
"You make it inkwich, boss," they said,
   "All same like Saltbush Bill."

They even said that they'd let him see
   The fires originate.
When he refused they said that he
   Was "No good magistrate".

And out beyond Sturt's Western track,
   And Leichhardt's farthest tree,
They wait till fate shall send them back
   Their Saltbush Bill, J.P.

RIDERS
IN THE STAND

THERE's some that ride the Robbo style, and bump at every stride;
While others sit a long way back, to get a longer ride.
There's some that ride as sailors do, with legs, and arms, and teeth;
And some ride on the horse's neck, and some ride underneath.

But all the finest horsemen out—the men to Beat the Band—
You'll find amongst the crowd that ride their races in the Stand.
They'll say "He had the race in hand, and lost it in the straight."
They'll show how Godby came too soon, and Barden came too late

They'll say Chevalley lost his nerve, and Regan lost his head;
They'll tell how one was "livened up" and something else was
        "dead"—
In fact, the race was never run on sea, or sky, or land,
But what you'd get it better done by riders in the Stand.

The rule holds good in everything in life's uncertain fight;
You'll find the winner can't go wrong, the loser can't go right.
You ride a slashing race, and lose—by one and all you're banned!
Ride like a bag of flour, and win—they'll cheer you in the Stand.

WALTZING
MATILDA
(Carrying a Swag.)

OH! there once was a swagman camped in a Billabong,
    Under the shade of a Coolabah tree;
And he sang as he looked at his old billy boiling,
    "Who'll come a-waltzing Matilda with me?"

      Who'll come a-waltzing Matilda, my darling,
        Who'll come a-waltzing Matilda with me?
      Waltzing Matilda and leading a water-bag—
        Who'll come a-waltzing Matilda with me?

Down came a jumbuck to drink at the water-hole,
    Up jumped the swagman and grabbed him in glee;
And he sang as he stowed him away in his tucker-bag,
    You'll come a-waltzing Matilda with me."

Down came the Squatter a-riding his thoroughbred;
    Down came Policemen—one, two and three.
      "Whose is the jumbuck you've got in the tucker-bag?
    You'll come a-waltzing Matilda with me."

But the swagman, he up and he jumped in the water-hole,
    Drowning himself by the Coolabah tree;
And his ghost may be heard as it sings in the Billabong
    "Who'll come a-waltzing Matilda with me?"

AN ANSWER
TO VARIOUS BARDS

WELL, I've waited mighty patient while they all came rolling in,
Mister Lawson, Mister Dyson, and the others of their kin,
With their dreadful, dismal stories of the Overlander's camp,
How his fire is always smoky, and his boots are always damp;
And they paint it so terrific it would fill one's soul with gloom—
But you know they're fond of writing about "corpses" and "the
        tomb".
So, before they curse the bushland, they should let their fancy range,
And take something for their livers, and be cheerful for a change.

Now, for instance, Mr Lawson—well, of course, we almost cried
At the sorrowful description how his "little 'Arvie" died,
And we lachrymosed in silence when "His Father's Mate" was slain;
Then he went and killed the father, and we had to weep again.
Ben Duggan and Jack Denver, too, he caused them to expire,
After which he cooked the gander of Jack Dunn, of Nevertire;
And, no doubt, the bush *is* wretched if you judge it by the groan
Of the sad and soulful poet with a graveyard of his own.

And he spoke in terms prophetic of a revolution's heat,
When the world should hear the clamour of those people in the
        street;
But the shearer chaps who start it—why, he rounds on them the
        blame,
And he calls 'em "agitators who are living on the game".
But I "over-write" the bushmen! Well, I own without a doubt
That I always see a hero in the "man from furthest out".
I could never contemplate him through an atmosphere of gloom,
And a bushman never struck me as a subject for "the tomb".

If it ain't all "golden sunshine" where the "wattle branches wave",
Well, it ain't all damp and dismal, and it ain't all "lonely grave".
And, of course, there's no denying that the bushman's life is rough,
But a man can easy stand it if he's built of sterling stuff;
Though it's seldom that the drover gets a bed of eiderdown,
Yet the man who's born a bushman, he gets mighty sick of town,
For he's jotting down the figures, and he's adding up the bills
While his heart is simply aching for a sight of Southern hills.

Then he hears a wool-team passing with a rumble and a lurch,
And, although the work is pressing, yet it brings him off his perch,
For it stirs him like a message from his station friends afar
And he seems to sniff the ranges in the scent of wool and tar;
And it takes him back in fancy, half in laughter, half in tears,
To a sound of other voices and a thought of other years,
When the woolshed rang with bustle from the dawning of the day,
And the shear-blades were a-clicking to the cry of "Wool away!"

Then his face was somewhat browner, and his frame was firmer set—
And he feels his flabby muscles with a feeling of regret.
But the wool-team slowly passes, and his eyes go sadly back
To the dusty little table and the papers in the rack,
And his thoughts go to the terrace where his sickly children squall,
And he thinks there's something healthy in the bush-life after all.
But we'll go no more a-droving in the wind or in the sun,
For our fathers' hearts have failed us, and the droving days are
      done.

There's a nasty dash of danger where the long-horned bullock
      wheels,
And we like to live in comfort and to get our reg'lar meals.
For to hang around the townships suits us better, you'll agree,
And a job at washing bottles is the job for such as we.
Let us herd into the cities, let us crush and crowd and push
Till we lose the love of roving, and we learn to hate the bush;
And we'll turn our aspirations to a city life and beer,
And we'll slip across to England—it's a nicer place than here;

For there's not much risk of hardship where all comforts are in
      store,
And the theatres are in plenty, and the pubs are more and more.
But that ends it, Mr Lawson, and it's time to say good-bye,
So we must agree to differ in all friendship, you and I.
Yes, we'll work our own salvation with the stoutest hearts we may,
And if fortune only favours we will take the road some day,
And go droving down the river 'neath the sunshine and the stars,
And then return to Sydney and vermilionize the bars.

T.Y.S.O.N.

Across the Queensland border line
    The mobs of cattle go;
They travel down in sun and shine
    On dusty stage, and slow.
The drovers, riding slowly on
    To let the cattle spread,
Will say: "Here's one old landmark gone,
    For old man Tyson's dead."

What tales there'll be in every camp
    By men that Tyson knew!
The swagmen, meeting on the tramp,
    Will yarn the long day through,
And tell of how he passed as "Brown",
    And fooled the local men:
"But not for me—I struck the town,
And passed the message further down;
    That's T.Y.S.O.N.!"

There stands a little country town
    Beyond the border line,
Where dusty roads go up and down,
    And banks with pubs combine.
A stranger came to cash a cheque—
    Few were the words he said—
A handkerchief about his neck,
    An old hat on his head.

A long grey stranger, eagle-eyed—
    "Know me? Of course you do?"
"It's not my work," the boss replied,
    "To know such tramps as you."
"Well, look here, Mister, don't be flash,"
    Replied the stranger then,
"I never care to make a splash,
I'm simple, but I've got the cash;
    I'm T.Y.S.O.N."

But in that last great drafting-yard,
    Where Peter keeps the gate,
And souls of sinners find it barred,
    And go to meet their fate,
There's one who ought to enter in
    For good deeds done on earth,
One who from Peter's self must win
    That meed of sterling worth.

Not to the strait and narrow gate
    Reserved for wealthy men,
But to the big gate, opened wide,
The grizzled figure, eagle-eyed,
    Will saunter up—and then
Old Peter'll say: "Let's pass him through;
There's many a thing he used to do,
Good-hearted things that no one knew;
    That's T.Y.S.O.N."

AS LONG AS YOUR EYES
ARE BLUE

"WILL you love me, sweet, when my hair is grey
  And my cheeks shall have lost their hue?
When the charms of youth shall have passed away
  Will your love as of old prove true?

"For the looks may change, and the heart may range
  And the love be no longer fond;
Will you love with truth in the years of youth
  And away to the years beyond?"

Oh, I love you, sweet, for your locks of brown
  And the blush on your cheek that lies—
But I love you most for the kindly heart
  That I see in your sweet blue eyes.

For the eyes are signs of the soul within,
  Of the heart that is leal and true,
And, my own sweetheart, I shall love you still,
  Just as long as your eyes are blue.

For the locks may bleach, and the cheeks of peach
  May be reft of their golden hue;
But, my own sweetheart, I shall love you still,
  Just as long as your eyes are blue.

BOTTLE-O!

I AIN'T the kind of bloke as takes to any steady job;
  I drives me bottle cart around the town;
A bloke what keeps 'is eyes about can always make a bob—
  I couldn't bear to graft for every brown.
There's lots of handy things about in everybody's yard,
  There's cocks and hens a-runnin' to an' fro,
And little dogs what comes and barks—we take 'em off their guard
  And we puts 'em with the Empty Bottle-O!

Chorus—

So it's any "Empty bottles! Any empty bottle-O!"
You can hear us round for half a mile or so.
  And you'll see the women rushing
  To take in the Monday's washing
When they 'ear us crying, "Empty Bottle-O!"

I'm driving down by Wexford-street and up a winder goes,
  A girl sticks out 'er 'ead and looks at me,
An all-right tart with ginger 'air, and freckles on 'er nose;
  I stops the cart and walks across to see.
"There ain't no bottles 'ere," says she, "since father took the pledge,"
  "No bottles 'ere," says I, "I'd like to know
What right 'ave you to stick your 'ead outside the winder ledge,
  If you 'aven't got no Empty Bottle-O!"

I sometimes gives the 'orse a spell, and then the push and me
  We takes a little trip to Chowder Bay.
Oh! ain't it nice the 'ole day long a-gazin' at the sea
  And a-hidin' of the tanglefoot away.
But when the booze gits 'old of us, and fellows starts to "scrap",
  There's some what likes blue-metal for to throw:
But as for me, I always says for layin' out a "trap"
  There's nothing like an Empty Bottle-O!

STORY OF
MONGREL GREY

THIS is the story the stockman told
  On the cattle-camp, when the stars were bright;
The moon rose up like a globe of gold
  And flooded the plain with her mellow light.
    We watched the cattle till dawn of day
    And he told me the story of Mongrel Grey.

He was a knock-about station hack,
  Spurred and walloped, and banged and beat;
Ridden all day with a sore on his back,
  Left all night with nothing to eat.
    That was a matter of everyday
    Normal occurrence with Mongrel Grey.

We might have sold him, but someone heard
  He was bred out back on a flooded run,
Where he learnt to swim like a waterbird;
  Midnight or midday were all as one—
    In the flooded ground he would find his way;
    Nothing could puzzle old Mongrel Grey.

'Tis a trick, no doubt, that some horses learn;
  When the floods are out they will splash along
In girth-deep water, and twist and turn
  From hidden channel and billabong,
    Never mistaking the road to go;
    For a man may guess—but the horses *know*.

I was camping out with my youngest son—
  Bit of a nipper, just learnt to speak—
In an empty hut on the lower run,
  Shooting and fishing in Conroy's Creek.
    The youngster toddled about all day
    And there with our horses was Mongrel Grey.

All of a sudden a flood came down,
  At first a freshet of mountain rain,
Roaring and eddying, rank and brown,
  Over the flats and across the plain.
    Rising and rising—at fall of night
    Nothing but water appeared in sight!

'Tis a nasty place when the floods are out,
  Even in daylight; for all around
Channels and billabongs twist about,
  Stretching for miles in the flooded ground.
    And to move seemed a hopeless thing to try
    In the dark with the storm-water racing by.

I had to risk it. I heard a roar
  As the wind swept down and the driving rain;
And the water rose till it reached the floor
  Of our highest room; and 'twas very plain—
    The way the torrent was sweeping down—
    We must make for the highlands at once, or drown

Off to the stable I splashed, and found
  The horses shaking with cold and fright;
I led them down to the lower ground,
  But never a yard would they swim that night!
    They reared and snorted and turned away,
    And none would face it but Mongrel Grey.

I bound the child on the horse's back,
  And we started off, with a prayer to heaven,
Through the rain and the wind and the pitchy black
  For I knew that the instinct God has given
    To prompt His creatures by night and day
    Would guide the footsteps of Mongrel Grey.

He struck deep water at once and swam—
  I swam beside him and held his mane—
Till we touched the bank of the broken dam
  In shallow water; then off again,
    Swimming in darkness across the flood,
    Rank with the smell of the drifting mud.

He turned and twisted across and back,
  Choosing the places to wade or swim,
Picking the safest and shortest track—
  The blackest darkness was clear to him.
    Did he strike the crossing by sight or smell?
    The Lord that held him alone could tell!

He dodged the timber whene'er he could,
  But timber brought us to grief at last;
I was partly stunned by a log of wood
  That struck my head as it drifted past;
    Then lost my grip of the brave old grey,
    And in half a second he swept away.

I reached a tree, where I had to stay,
  And did a perish for two days' hard;
And lived on water—but Mongrel Grey,
  He walked right into the homestead yard
    At dawn next morning, and grazed around,
    With the child strapped on to him safe and sound.

We keep him now for the wife to ride,
  Nothing too good for him now, of course;
Never a whip on his fat old hide,
  For she owes the child to that brave grey horse.
    And not Old Tyson himself could pay
    The purchase money of Mongrel Grey.

GILHOOLEY'S ESTATE

(A ballad concerning the amalgamation of the legal profession.)

OH, Mr Gilhooley he turned up his toes,
  As most of us do, soon or late;
And Jones was a lawyer, as everyone knows,
  So they took him Gilhooley's Estate.

Gilhooley in life had been living so free
  'Twas thought his possessions were great,
So Jones, with a smile, says, "There's many a fee
  For me in Gilhooley's Estate."

They made out a list of his property fine,
  It totalled a thousand-and-eight;
But the debts. were nine hundred and ninety nine—
  The debts of Gilhooley's Estate.

So Mrs Gilhooley says, "Jones, my dear man,
  My childer have little to ait:
Just keep the expinses as low as you can
  Against poor Gilhooley's Estate."

But Jones says, "The will isn't clear in its terms,
  I fear it will need some debate,
And the law won't allow me (attorneys are worms)
  To appear in Gilhooley's Estate."

So a barrister-man, with a wig on his head
  And a brief in his hand, quite elate,
Went up to the Court where they bury the dead,
  Just to move in Gilhooley's Estate.

But his Honour the Judge said, "I think that the joint
  Legatees must be called to *probate*—
Ex parte Pokehorney is clear on the point—
  The point of Gilhooley's Estate."

"I order a suit to be brought just to try
  If this is correct that I state—
A nice friendly suit—and the costs by and by,
  Must be borne by Gilhooley's Estate."

So Mrs Gilhooley says, "Jones, you'll appear!
    Thim barristers' fees is too great;
The suit is but friendly," "Attorneys, my dear,
    Can't be heard in Gilhooley's Estate."

From the barristers' quarter a mighty hurrah
    Arises both early and late:
It's only the whoop of the Junior Bar
    Dividing Gilhooley's Estate.

"But, when the dawn makes pink the sky . . .", from *Brumby's Run*—
the frontispiece prepared by Lionel Lindsay for
Saltbush Bill, J.P.

THE ROAD
TO HOGAN'S GAP

Now look, you see, it's this way like—
  You cross the broken bridge
And run the crick down, till you strike
  The second right-hand ridge.

The track is hard to see in parts,
  But still it's pretty clear;
There's been two Injun hawkers' carts
  Along that road this year.

Well, run that right-hand ridge along—
  It ain't, to say, too steep—
There's two fresh tracks might put you wrong
  Where blokes went out with sheep.

But keep the crick upon your right,
  And follow pretty straight
Along the spur, until you sight
  A wire and sapling gate.

Well, that's where Hogan's old grey mare
  Fell off and broke her back;
You'll see her carcass layin' there,
  Jist down below the track.

And then you drop two mile, or three,
  It's pretty steep and blind;
You want to go and fall a tree
  And tie it on behind.

And then you pass a broken cart
  Below a granite bluff;
And that is where you strike the part
  They reckon pretty rough.

But by the time you've got that far
  It's either cure or kill,
So turn your horses round the spur
  And face 'em up the hill.

For look, if you should miss the slope
  And get below the track,
You haven't got the slightest hope
  Of ever gettin' back.

An' half way up you'll see the hide
  Of Hogan's brindled bull;
Well, mind and keep the right-hand side.
  The left's too steep a pull.

And both the banks is full of cracks;
  An' just about at dark
You'll see the last year's bullock tracks
  Where Hogan drew the bark.

The marks is old and pretty faint—
  O'ergrown with scrub and such;
Of course the track to Hogan's ain't
  A road that's travelled much.

But turn and run the tracks along
  For half a mile or more,
And then, of course, you can't go wrong—
  You're right at Hogan's door.

When first you come to Hogan's gate
  He mightn't show perhaps;
He's pretty sure to plant, and wait
  To see it ain't the traps.

I wouldn't call it good enough
  To let your horses out;
There's some that's pretty extra rough
  Is livin' round about.

It's likely, if your horses did
  Get feedin' near the track,
It's going to cost at least a quid
  Or more to get them back.

So, if you find they're off the place,
  It's up to you to go
And flash a quid in Hogan's face—
  He'll know the blokes that know.

But listen—if you're feelin' dry,
  Just see there's no one near,
And go and wink the other eye
  And ask for ginger beer.

The blokes come in from near and far
  To sample Hogan's pop;
They reckon once they breast the bar
  They stay there till they drop.

On Sundays you can see them spread
  Like flies around the tap.
It's like that song "The Livin' Dead"
  Up there at Hogan's Gap.

They like to make it pretty strong
  Whenever there's a chance;
So when a stranger comes along
  They always hold a dance.

There's recitations, songs, and fights—
  A willin' lot you'll meet.
There's one long bloke up there recites;
  I tell you he's a treat.

They're lively blokes all right up there,
  It's never dull a day.
I'd go meself if I could spare
  The time to get away.

          .   .   .   .   .

The stranger turned his horses quick.
  He didn't cross the bridge;
He didn't go along the crick
  To strike the second ridge;

He didn't make the trip, because
  He wasn't feeling fit.
His business up at Hogan's was
  To serve him with a writ.

He reckoned, if he faced the pull
  And climbed the rocky stair,
The next to come might find his hide
A landmark on the mountain side,
Along with Hogan's brindled bull
  And Hogan's old grey mare!

A SINGER OF
THE BUSH

THERE is waving of grass in the breeze
  And a song in the air,
And a murmur of myriad bees
  That toil everywhere.
There is scent in the blossom and bough,
  And the breath of the Spring
Is as soft as a kiss on a brow—
  And Springtime I sing.

There is drought on the land, and the stock
  Tumble down in their tracks
Or follow—a tottering flock—
  The scrub-cutter's axe.
While ever a creature survives
  The axes shall swing;
We are fighting with fate for their lives—
  And the combat I sing.

"SHOUTING" FOR
A CAMEL

It was over at Coolgardie that a mining speculator,
    Who was going down the township just to make a bit o' chink,
Went off to hire a camel from a camel propagator,
    And the Afghan said he'd lend it if he'd stand the beast a drink.
Yes, the only price he asked him was to stand the beast a drink.
He was cheap, very cheap, as the dromedaries go.

So the mining speculator made the bargain, proudly thinking
    He had bested old Mahomet, he had done him in the eye.
Then he clambered on the camel, and the while the beast was
        drinking
    He explained with satisfaction to the miners standing by
That 'twas cheap, very cheap, as the dromedaries go.

But the camel kept on drinking and he filled his hold with water,
    And the more he had inside him yet the more he seemed to need;
For he drank it by the gallon, and his girths grew taut and tauter,
    And the miners muttered softly, "Yes he's very dry indeed!
But he's cheap, very cheap, as the dromedaries go."

So he drank up twenty buckets—it was weird to watch him suck it,
    (And the market price for water was per bucket half-a-crown)
Till the speculator stopped him, saying, "Not another bucket—
    If I give him any more there'll be a famine in the town.
Take him back to old Mahomet, and I'll tramp it through the
        town."
He was cheap, very cheap, as the speculators go.

There's a moral to this story—in your hat you ought to paste it—
    Be careful whom you shout for when a camel is about,
And there's plenty human camels who, before they'll see you
        waste it,
    Will drink up all you pay for if you're fool enough to shout;
If you chance to strike a camel when you're fool enough to shout,
You'll be cheap, very cheap, as the speculators go.

MULLIGAN'S
MARE

Oh, Mulligan's bar was the deuce of a place
To drink, and to fight, and to gamble and race;
The height of choice spirits from near and from far
Were all concentrated on Mulligan's bar.

There was "Jerry the Swell", and the jockey-boy Ned,
"Dog-bite-me"—so called from the shape of his head—
And a man whom the boys, in their musical slang,
Designated the "Gaffer of Mulligan's Gang".

Now Mulligan's Gang had a racer to show,
A bad un to look at, a good un to go;
Whenever they backed her you safely might swear
She'd walk in a winner, would Mulligan's mare.

But Mulligan, having some radical views,
Neglected his business and got on the booze;
He took up with runners—a treacherous troop—
Who gave him away, and he "fell in the soup".

And so it turned out on a fine summer day,
A bailiff turned up with a writ of "*fi. fa.*";
He walked to the bar with a manner serene,
"I levy," said he, "in the name of the Queen."

Then Mulligan wanted, in spite of the law,
To pay out the bailiff with "*one* on the jaw";
He drew out to hit him; but ere you could wink,
He changed his intention and stood him a drink.

A great consultation there straightway befell
'Twixt jockey-boy Neddy and Jerry the Swell,
And the man with the head, who remarked "Why, you bet!
Dog-bite-me!" said he, "but we'll diddle 'em yet.

"We'll slip out the mare from her stall in a crack,
And put in her place the old broken-down hack;
The hack is so like her, I'm ready to swear
The bailiff will think he has Mulligan's mare.

"So out with the racer and in with the screw,
We'll show him what Mulligan's talent can do;
And if he gets nasty and dares to say much,
I'll knock him as stiff as my grandmother's crutch."

Then off to the town went the mare and the lad;
The bailiff came out, never dreamt he was "had";
But marched to the stall with a confident air—
"I levy," said he, "upon Mulligan's mare."

He watched her by day and he watched her by night,
She was never an instant let out of his sight,
For races were coming away in the West
And Mulligan's mare had a chance with the best.

"Here's a slant," thought the bailiff, "to serve my own ends,
I'll send off a wire to my bookmaking friends:
'Get all you can borrow, beg, snavel or snare
And lay the whole lot against Mulligan's mare.'"

The races came round, and the crowd on the course
Were laying the mare till they made themselves hoarse,
And Mulligan's party, with ardour intense,
They backed her for pounds and for shillings and pence.

But think of the grief of the bookmaking host
At the sound of the summons to go to the post—
For down to the start with her thoroughbred air
As fit as a fiddle pranced Mulligan's mare!

They started, and off went the boy to the front,
He cleared out at once, and he made it a hunt;
He steadied as rounding the corner they wheeled,
Then gave her her head—and she smothered the field.

The race put her owner right clear of his debts;
He landed a fortune in stakes and in bets,
He paid the old bailiff the whole of his pelf,
And gave him a hiding to keep for himself.

So all you bold sportsmen take warning, I pray,
Keep clear of the running, you'll find it don't pay;
For the very best rule that you'll hear in a week
Is never to bet on a thing that can speak.

And, whether you're lucky or whether you lose,
Keep clear of the cards and keep clear of the booze,
And fortune in season will answer your prayer
And send you a flyer like Mulligan's mare.

THE MOUNTAIN SQUATTER

HERE in my mountain home,
  On rugged hills and steep,
I sit and watch you come,
  O Riverina Sheep!

You come from fertile plains
  Where saltbush (sometimes) grows,
And flats that (when it rains)
  Will blossom like the rose.

But when the summer sun
  Gleams down like burnished brass,
You have to leave your run
  And hustle off for grass.

'Tis then that—forced to roam—
  You come to where I keep,
Here in my mountain home,
  A boarding-house for sheep.

Around me where I sit
  The wary wombat goes—
A beast of little wit,
  But what he knows, he *knows*.

The very same remark
  Applies to me also;
I don't give out a spark,
  But what I know, I *know*.

My brain perhaps would show
  No convolutions deep,
But anyhow I know
  The way to handle sheep.

These Riverina cracks,
  They do not care to ride
The half-inch hanging tracks
  Along the mountain side.

Their horses shake with fear
　　When loosened boulders go
With leaps, like startled deer,
　　Down to the gulfs below.

Their very dogs will shirk,
　　And drop their tails in fright
When asked to go and work
　　A mob that's out of sight.

My little collie pup
　　Works silently and wide;
You'll see her climbing up
　　Along the mountain side.

As silent as a fox
　　You'll see her come and go,
A shadow through the rocks
　　Where ash and messmate grow.

Then, lost to sight and sound
　　Behind some rugged steep,
She works her way around
　　And gathers up the sheep;

And, working wide and shy,
　　She holds them rounded up.
The cash ain't coined to buy
　　That little collie pup.

And so I draw a screw
　　For self and dog and keep
To boundary-ride for you,
　　O Riverina Sheep!

And, when the autumn rain
　　Has made the herbage grow,
You travel off again,
　　And glad—no doubt—to go.

But some are left behind
　　Around the mountain's spread,
For those we cannot find
　　We put them down as dead.

So, when we say adieu
  And close the boarding job,
I always find a few
  Fresh ear-marks in my mob.

And, what with those I sell,
  And what with those I keep,
You pay me pretty well,
  O Riverina Sheep!

It's up to me to shout
  Before we say good-bye—
"Here's to a howlin' drought
  All west of Gundagai!"

PIONEERS

THEY came of bold and roving stock that would not fixed abide;
They were the sons of field and flock since e'er they learnt to ride,
We may not hope to see such men in these degenerate years
As those explorers of the bush—the brave old pioneers.

'Twas they who rode the trackless bush in heat and storm and
        drought;
'Twas they who heard the master-word that called them farther
        out;
'Twas they who followed up the trail the mountain cattle made,
And pressed across the mighty range where now their bones are laid.

But now the times are dull and slow, the brave old days are dead
When hardy bushmen started out, and forced their way ahead
By tangled scrub and forests grim towards the unknown west,
And spied at last the promised land from off the range's crest.

O ye that sleep in lonely graves by distant ridge and plain,
We drink to you in silence now as Christmas comes again,
To you who fought the wilderness through rough unsettled years—
The founders of our nation's life, the brave old pioneers.

SANTA CLAUS
IN THE BUSH

It chanced out back at the Christmas time,
   When the wheat was ripe and tall,
A stranger rode to the farmer's gate—
   A sturdy man and a small.

"Rin doon, rin doon, my little son Jack,
   And bid the stranger stay;
And we'll hae a crack for Auld Lang Syne,
   For the morn is Christmas Day."

"Nay noo, nay noo," said the dour guidwife,
   "But ye should let him be;
He's maybe only a drover chap
   Frae the land o' the Darling Pea.

"Wi' a drover's tales, and a drover's thirst
   To swiggle the hail nicht through;
Or he's maybe a life assurance carle
   To talk ye black and blue."

"Guidwife, he's never a drover chap,
   For their swags are neat and thin;
And he's never a life assurance carle,
   Wi' the brick-dust burnt in his skin.

"Guidwife, guidwife, be nae sae dour,
   For the wheat stands ripe and tall,
And we shore a seven-pound fleece this year,
   Ewes and weaners and all.

"There is grass tae spare, and the stock are fat.
   Where they whiles are gaunt and thin,
And we owe a tithe to the travelling poor,
   So we maun ask him in.

"Ye can set him a chair tae the table side,
   And gi' him a bite tae eat;
An omelette made of a new-laid egg,
   Or a tasty bit of meat."

"But the native cats have taen the fowls,
　　They havena left a leg;
And he'll get nae omelette at a'
　　Till the emu lays an egg!"

"Rin doon, rin doon, my little son Jack,
　　To whaur the emus bide,
Ye shall find the auld hen on the nest,
　　While the auld cock sits beside.

"But speak them fair, and speak them saft,
　　Lest they kick ye a fearsome jolt.
Ye can gi' them a feed of thae half-inch nails
　　Or a rusty carriage bolt."

So little son Jack ran blithely down
　　With the rusty nails in hand,
Till he came where the emus fluffed and scratched
　　By their nest in the open sand.

And there he has gathered the new-laid egg—
　　'Twould feed three men or four—
And the emus came for the half-inch nails
　　Right up to the settler's door.

"A waste o' food," said the dour guidwife,
　　As she took the egg, with a frown,
"But he gets nae meat, unless ye rin
　　A paddy-melon down."

"Gang oot, gang oot, my little son Jack,
　　Wi' your twa-three doggies sma';
Gin ye come nae back wi' a paddy-melon,
　　Then come nae back at a'."

So little son Jack he raced and he ran,
　　And he was bare o' the feet,
And soon he captured a paddy-melon,
　　Was gorged with the stolen wheat.

"Sit doon, sit doon, my bonny wee man,
　　To the best that the hoose can do—
An omelette made of the emu egg
　　And a paddy-melon stew."

" 'Tis well, 'tis well," said the bonny wee man;
  "I have eaten the wide world's meat,
And the food that is given with right good-will
  Is the sweetest food to eat.

"But the night draws on to the Christmas Day
  And I must rise and go,
For I have a mighty way to ride
  To the land of the Esquimaux.

"And it's there I must load my sledges up,
  With the reindeers four-in-hand,
That go to the North, South, East, and West,
  To every Christian land."

"Tae the Esquimaux," said the dour guidwife,
  "Ye suit my husband well!
For when he gets up on his journey horse
  He's a bit of a liar himsel'."

Then out with a laugh went the bonny wee man
  To his old horse grazing nigh,
And away like a meteor flash they went
  Far off to the Northern sky.

        .   .   .   .   .   .

When the children woke on the Christmas morn
  They chattered with might and main—
For a sword and gun had little son Jack,
  And a braw new doll had Jane,
And a packet o' screws had the twa emus;
  But the dour guidwife gat nane.

239

"IN RE
A GENTLEMAN, ONE"

*When an attorney is called before the Full Court to
answer for any alleged misconduct it is not usual
to publish his name until he is found guilty; until
then the matter appears in the papers as "In re
a Gentleman, One of the Attorneys of the Supreme
Court," or, more shortly, "In re a Gent., One."*

WE see it each day in the paper,
   And know that there's mischief in store;
That some unprofessional caper
   Has landed a shark on the shore.
We know there'll be plenty of trouble
   Before they get through with the fun,
Because he's been coming the double
   On clients, has "Gentleman, One".

Alas for the gallant attorney,
   Intent upon cutting a dash!
He starts on life's perilous journey
   With rather more cunning than cash.
And fortune at first is inviting—
   He struts his brief hour in the sun—
But, lo! on the wall is the writing
   Of Nemesis, "Gentleman, One".

For soon he runs short of the dollars,
   He fears he must go to the wall;
So Peters' trust-money he collars
   To pay off his creditor, Paul;
Then robs right and left—for he goes it
   In earnest when once he's begun.
Descensus Averni—he knows it;
   It's easy for "Gentleman, One".

The crash comes as sure as the seasons,
   He loses his coin in a mine,
Or booming in land, or for reasons
   Connected with women and wine.

Or maybe the cards or the horses
  A share of the damage have done—
No matter; the end of the course is
  The same: "*Re* a Gentleman, One."

He struggles awhile to keep going,
  To stave off detection and shame;
But creditors, clamorous growing,
  Ere long put an end to the game.
At length the poor soldier of Satan
  His course to a finish has run—
And just think of Windeyer waiting
  To deal with "A Gentleman, One"!

And some face it boldly, and brazen
  The shame and the utter disgrace;
While others, more sensitive, hasten
  Their names and their deeds to efface.
They snap the frail thread which the Furies
  And Fates have so cruelly spun.
May the great Final Judge and His juries
  Have mercy on "Gentleman, One"!

AT THE MELTING OF THE SNOW

THERE'S a sunny Southern land,
  And it's there that I would be
Where the big hills stand,
  In the South Countrie!
When the wattles bloom again,
  Then it's time for us to go
To the old Monaro country
  At the melting of the snow.

To the East or to the West,
  Or wherever you may be,
You will find no place
  Like the South Countrie.
For the skies are blue above,
  And the grass is green below,
In the old Monaro country
  At the melting of the snow.

Now the team is in the plough,
  And the thrushes start to sing,
And the pigeons on the bough
  Sit a-welcoming the Spring.
So come, my comrades all,
  Let us saddle up and go
To the old Monaro country
  At the melting of the snow.

A DREAM OF
THE MELBOURNE CUP

(1886)

BRING me a quart of colonial beer
And some doughy damper to make good cheer,
  I must make a heavy dinner;
Heavily dine and heavily sup,
Of indigestible things fill up,
Next month they run the Melbourne Cup,
  And I have to dream the winner.

Stoke it in, boys! the half-cooked ham,
The rich ragout and the charming cham.,
  I've got to mix my liquor;
Give me a gander's gaunt hind leg,
Hard and tough as a wooden peg,
And I'll keep it down with a hard-boiled egg,
  'Twill make me dream the quicker.

Now that I'm full of fearful feed,
Oh, but I'll dream of a winner indeed
  In my restless, troubled slumber;
While the night-mares race through my heated brain
And their devil-riders spur amain,
The trip for the Cup will reward my pain,
  And I'll spot the winning number.

Thousands and thousands and thousands more,
Like sands on the white Pacific shore,
  The crowding people cluster;
For evermore is the story old,
While races are bought and backers are sold,
Drawn by the greed of the gain of gold,
  In their thousands still they muster.

    .   .   .   .   .

And the bookies' cries grow fierce and hot,
"I'll lay the Cup! The double, if not!"
  "Five monkeys, Little John, sir!"
"Here's fives bar one, I lay, I lay!"
And so they shout through the livelong day,
And stick to the game that is sure to pay,
  While fools put money on, sir!

And now in my dream I seem to go
And bet with a "book" that I seem to know—
　　A Hebrew money-lender;
A million to five is the price I get—
Not bad! but before I book the bet
The horse's name I clean forget,
　　Its number and even gender.

Now for the start, and here they come,
And the hoof-strokes roar like a mighty drum
　　Beat by a hand unsteady;
They come like a rushing, roaring flood,
Hurrah for the speed of the Chester blood;
For Acme is making the pace so good
　　They are some of 'em done already.

But round the back she begins to tire,
And a mighty shout goes up "Crossfire!"
　　The magpie jacket's leading;
And Crossfire challenges, fierce and bold,
And the lead she'll have and the lead she'll hold,
But at length gives way to the black and gold,
　　Which right to the front is speeding.

Carry them on and keep it up—
A flying race is the Melbourne Cup,
　　You must race and stay to win it;
And old Commotion, Victoria's pride,
Now takes the lead with his raking stride,
And a mighty roar goes far and wide—
　　"There's only Commotion in it!"

But one draws out from the beaten ruck
And up on the rails by a piece of luck
　　He comes in a style that's clever;
"It's Trident! Trident! Hurrah for Hales!"
"Go at 'em now while their courage fails;"
"Trident! Trident! for New South Wales!"
　　"The blue and white for ever!"

Under the whip! with the ears flat back,
Under the whip! though the sinews crack,
　　No sign of the base white feather:

Stick to it now for your breeding's sake,
Stick to it now though your hearts should break,
While the yells and roars make the grand-stand shake,
    They come down the straight together.

Trident slowly forges ahead,
The fierce whips cut and the spurs are red,
    The pace is undiminished
Now for the Panics that never fail!
But many a backer's face grows pale
As old Commotion swings his tail
    And swerves—and the Cup is finished.

            .   .   .   .   .   .

And now in my dream it all comes back:
I bet my coin on the Sydney crack,
    A million I've won, no question!
"Give me my money, you hook-nosed hog!
Give me my money, bookmaking dog!"
But he disappeared in a kind of fog,
    And I woke with "the indigestion".

THE GUNDAROO BULLOCK

Oh, there's some that breeds the Devon that's as solid as a stone,
And there's some that breeds the brindle which they call the
    "Goulburn Roan";
But amongst the breeds of cattle there are very, very few
Like the hairy-whiskered bullock that they bred at Gundaroo.

Far away by Grabben Gullen, where the Murrumbidgee flows,
There's a block of broken country-side where no one ever goes;
For the banks have gripped the squatters, and the free selectors too,
And their stock are always stolen by the men of Gundaroo.

There came a low informer to the Grabben Gullen side,
And he said to Smith the squatter, "You must saddle up and ride,
For your bullock's in the harness-cask of Morgan Donahoo—
He's the greatest cattle-stealer in the whole of Gundaroo."

"Oh, ho!" said Smith, the owner of the Grabben Gullen run,
"I'll go and get the troopers by the sinking of the sun,
And down into his homestead tonight we'll take a ride,
With warrants to identify the carcass and the hide."

That night rode down the troopers, the squatter at their head,
They rode into the homestead, and pulled Morgan out of bed.
"Now, show to us the carcass of the bullock that you slew—
The hairy-whiskered bullock that you killed in Gundaroo."

They peered into the harness-cask, and found it wasn't full,
But down among the brine they saw some flesh and bits of wool.
"What's this?" exclaimed the trooper; "an infant, I declare;"
Said Morgan. "'Tis the carcass of an old man native bear.
I heard that ye were coming, so an old man bear I slew,
Just to give you kindly welcome to my home in Gundaroo.

"The times are something awful, as you can plainly see,
The banks have broke the squatters, and they've broke the likes
    of me;
We can't afford a bullock—such expense would never do—
So an old man bear for breakfast is a treat in Gundaroo."
And along by Grabben Gullen, where the rushing river flows,
In the block of broken country where there's no one ever goes,
On the Upper Murrumbidgee, they're a hospitable crew—
But you mustn't ask for "bullock" when you go to Gundaroo.

LAY OF
THE MOTOR-CAR

WE'RE away! and the wind whistles shrewd
    In our whiskers and teeth;
And the granite-like grey of the road
    Seems to slide underneath.
As an eagle might sweep through the sky,
    So we sweep through the land;
And the pallid pedestrians fly
    When they hear us at hand.

We outpace, we outlast, we outstrip!
    Not the fast-fleeing hare,
Nor the racehorses under the whip,
    Nor the birds of the air
Can compete with our swiftness sublime,
    Our ease and our grace.
We annihilate chickens and time
    And policemen and space.

Do you mind that fat grocer who crossed?
    How he dropped down to pray
In the road when he saw he was lost;
    How he melted away
Underneath, and there rang through the fog
    His earsplitting squeal
As he went——Is that he or a dog,
    That stuff on the wheel?

THE
CORNER-MAN

I DREAMT a dream at the midnight deep,
  When fancies come and go
To vex a man in his soothing sleep
  With thoughts of awful woe—
I dreamt that I was a corner-man
  Of a nigger minstrel show.

I cracked my jokes, and the building rang
  With laughter loud and long;
I hushed the house as I softly sang
  An old plantation song—
A tale of the wicked slavery days
  Of cruelty and wrong.

A small boy sat on the foremost seat—
  A mirthful youngster he;
He beat the time with his restless feet
  To each new melody,
And he picked me out as the brightest star
  Of the black fraternity.

"Oh father," he said, "what *would* we do
  If the corner-man should die?
I never saw such a man—did you?
  He makes the people cry,
And then, when he likes, he makes them laugh.
  The old man made reply—

"We each of us fill a very small space
  In the great creation's plan,
If a man don't keep his lead in the race
  There's plenty more that can;
The world can very soon fill the place
  Of even a corner-man."

   ·   ·   ·   ·   ·   ·

I woke with a jump, rejoiced to find
  Myself at home in bed,
And I framed a moral in my mind
  From the words the old man said.
The world will jog along just the same
  When its corner-men are dead.

WHEN DACEY
RODE THE MULE

'TWAS to a small, up-country town,
  When we were boys at school,
There came a circus with a clown,
  Likewise a bucking mule.
The clown announced a scheme they had
  Spectators for to bring—
They'd give a crown to any lad
  Who'd ride him round the ring.

    And, gentle reader, do not scoff
      Nor think a man a fool—
    To buck a porous-plaster off
      Was pastime to that mule.

The boys got on he bucked like sin;
  He threw them in the dirt.
What time the clown would raise a grin
  By asking, "Are you hurt?"
But Johnny Dacey came one night,
  The crack of all the school;
Said he, "I'll win the crown all right;
  Bring in your bucking mule."

    The elephant went off his trunk,
      The monkey played the fool,
    And all the band got blazing drunk
      When Dacey rode the mule.

But soon there rose a galling shout
  Of laughter, for the clown
From somewhere in his pants drew out
  A little paper crown.
He placed the crown on Dacey's head
  While Dacey looked a fool;
"Now, there's your crown, my lad," he said,
  "For riding of the mule!"

    The band struck up with "Killaloe",
      And "Rule Britannia, Rule",
    And "Young Man from the Country", too,
      When Dacey rode the mule.

Then Dacey, in a furious rage,
  For vengeance on the show
Ascended to the monkeys' cage
  And let the monkeys go;
The blue-tailed ape and the chimpanzee
  He turned abroad to roam;
Good faith! It was a sight to see
  The people step for home.

    For big baboons with canine snout
      Are spiteful, as a rule—
    The people didn't sit it out,
      When Dacey rode the mule.

And from the beasts he let escape,
  The bushmen all declare,
Were born some creatures partly ape
  And partly native-bear.
They're rather few and far between,
  The race is nearly spent;
But some of them may still be seen
  In Sydney Parliament.

    And when those legislators fight,
      And drink, and act the fool,
    Just blame it on that torrid night
      When Dacey rode the mule.

THE MYLORA
ELOPEMENT

By the winding Wollondilly where the weeping willows weep,
And the shepherd, with his billy, half awake and half asleep,
Folds his fleecy flocks that linger homewards in the setting sun
Lived my hero, Jim the Ringer, "cocky" on Mylora Run.

Jimmy loved the super's daughter, Miss Amelia Jane McGrath.
Long and earnestly he sought her, but he feared her stern papa;
And Amelia loved him truly—but the course of love, if true,
Never yet ran smooth or duly, as I think it ought to do.

Pondering o'er his predilection, Jimmy watched McGrath, the boss,
Riding past his lone selection, looking for a station 'oss
That was running in the ranges with a mob of outlaws wild.
Mac the time of day exchanges—off goes Jim to see his child;

Says, "The old man's after Stager, which he'll find is no light job,
And tomorrow I will wager he will try and yard the mob.
Will you come with me tomorrow? I will let the parson know,
And for ever, joy or sorrow, he will join us here below.

"I will bring my nags so speedy, Crazy Jane and Tambourine,
One more kiss—don't think I'm greedy—good-bye, lass, before I'm
       seen—
Just one more—God bless you, dearie! Don't forget to meet me here,
Life without you is but weary; now, once more, good-bye, my dear."

·   ·   ·   ·   ·

The daylight shines on figures twain
That ride across Mylora plain,
Laughing and talking—Jim and Jane.
"Steadily, darling. There's lots of time,
Didn't we slip the old man prime!
I knew he'd tackle that Bowneck mob,
I reckon he'll find it too big a job.
They've beaten us all. I had a try,
But the warrigal devils seem to fly.
That Sambo's a real good bit of stuff
No doubt, but not quite good enough.

251

He'll have to gallop the livelong day,
To cut and come, to race and stay.
I hope he yards 'em, 'twill do him good;
To see us going I don't think would."
A turn in the road and, fair and square,
They meet the old man standing there.
"What's up?" "Why, running away, of course,"
Says Jim, emboldened. The old man turned,
His eye with wild excitement burned.
"I've raced all day through the scorching heat
After old Bowneck: and now I'm beat.
But over that range I think you'll find
The Bowneck mob all run stone-blind.
Will you go, and leave the mob behind?
Which will you do? Take the girl away,
Or ride like a white man should today,
And yard old Bowneck? Go or stay?
Says Jim, "I can't throw this away,
We can bolt some other day, of course—
Amelia Jane, get off that horse!
Up you get, Old Man. Whoop, halloo!
Here goes to put old Bowneck through!"
Two distant specks on the mountain side,
Two stockwhips echoing far and wide. . . .
Amelia Jane sat down and cried.

     ·   ·   ·   ·   ·   ·

"Sakes, Amelia, what's up now?
Leading old Sambo, too, I vow,
And him deadbeat. Where have you been?
'Bolted with Jim!' What *do* you mean?
'Met the old man with Sambo, licked
From running old Bowneck.' Well, I'm kicked—
'Ran 'em till Sambo nearly dropped?'
What did Jim do when you were stopped?
Did you bolt from father across the plain?
'Jim made you get off Crazy Jane!
And father got on, and away again
The two of 'em went to the ranges grim.'
Good boy, Jimmy! Oh, well done, Jim!
They're sure to get them now, of course,

That Tambourine is a spanking horse.
And Crazy Jane is good as gold.
And Jim, they say, rides pretty bold—
Not like your father, but very fair.
Jim will have to follow the mare."
"It never was yet in father's hide
To best my Jim on the mountain side.
Jim can rally, and Jim can ride."
But here again Amelia cried.

   .   .   .   .   .   .

The sound of a whip comes faint and far,
A rattle of hoofs, and here they are,
In all their tameless pride.
The fleet wild horses snort with fear,
And wheel and break as the yard draws near.
Now, Jim the Ringer, ride!
Wheel 'em! wheel 'em! Whoa back there, whoa!
And the foam-flakes fly like the driven snow,
As under the whip the horses go
Adown the mountain side.
And Jim, hands down, and teeth firm set,
On a horse that never has failed him yet,
Is after them down the range.
Well ridden! well ridden! they wheel—whoa back!
And long and loud the stockwhips crack,
Their flying course they change;
"Steadily does it—let Sambo go!
Open those sliprails down below.
Smart! or you'll be too late.

   .   .   .   .   .   .

"They'll follow old Sambo up—look out!
Wheel that black horse—give Sam a clout.
They're in! Make fast the gate."

   .   .   .   .   .   .

The mob is safely in the yard!
The old man mounts delighted guard.
No thought has he but for his prize.

   .   .   .   .   .   .

Jim catches poor Amelia's eyes.
"Will you come after all? The job is done,
And Crazy Jane is fit to run
For a prince's life—now don't say no;
Slip on while the old man's down below
At the inner yard, and away we'll go.
Will you come, my girl?" "I will, you bet;
We'll manage this here elopement yet."

· · · · · ·

By the winding Wollondilly stands the hut of Ringer Jim.
And his loving little Meely makes a perfect god of him.
He has stalwart sons and daughters, and, I think, before he's done,
There'll be numerous "Six-fortys" taken on Mylora run.

THE PANNIKIN POET

THERE'S nothing here sublime,
But just a roving rhyme,
Run off to pass the time,
    With nought titanic in.
The theme that it supports,
And, though it treats of quarts,
It's bare of golden thoughts—
    It's just a pannikin.

I think it's rather hard
That each Australian bard—
Each wan, poetic card—
    With thoughts galvanic in
His fiery soul alight,
In wild aerial flight,
Will sit him down and write
    About a pannikin.

He makes some new-chum fare
From out his English lair
To hunt the native bear,
    That curious mannikin;
And then when times get bad
That wandering English lad
Writes out a message sad
    Upon his pannikin:

"O mother, think of me
Beneath the wattle tree"
(For you may bet that he
    Will drag the wattle in)
"O mother, here I think
That I shall have to sink,
There ain't a single drink
    The water-bottle in."

The dingo homeward hies,
The sooty crows uprise
And caw their fierce surprise
    A tone Satanic in;
And bearded bushmen tread
Around the sleeper's head—
"See here—the bloke is dead!
    Now where's his pannikin?"

They read his words and weep,
And lay him down to sleep
Where wattle-branches sweep,
    A style mechanic in;
And, reader, that's the way
The poets of today
Spin out their little lay
    About a pannikin.

THE
PROTEST

I SAY 'e *isn't* Remorse!
  'Ow do I know?
Saw 'im on Riccarton course
  Two year ago!
Think I'd forget any 'orse?
  Course 'e's The Crow!

Bumper Maginnis and I
  After a "go",
Walkin' our 'orses to dry,
  I says "Hello!
What's that old black goin' by?"
  Bumper says "Oh!
That's an old cuddy of Flanagan's—
  Runs as The Crow!"

Now they make out 'e's Remorse.
  Well, but I *know*.
Soon as I came on the course
  I says " 'Ello!
'Ere's the old Crow."
Once a man's seen any 'orse,
  Course 'e must know.
Sure as there's wood in this table,
  I say 'e's The Crow.

(Cross-examined by the Committee.)
  'Ow do I know the moke
    After one sight?
S'posin' you meet a bloke
  Down town at night,
Wouldn't you know 'im again when you met 'im?
  That's *'im* all right!

What was the brand on 'is 'ide?
  I couldn't say,
Brands can be transmogrified.
  That ain't the way—
It's the *look* of a 'orse and the way that 'e moves
  That I'd know any day.

What was the boy on 'is back?
  Why, 'e went past
All of a minute, and off down the track.
  —"The 'orse went as fast?"
True, so 'e did! But, my eyes, what a treat!
'Ow can I notice the 'ands and the seat
Of each bumble-faced kid of a boy that I meet?
  Lor'! What a question to ast!
  (Protest Dismissed.)

AN EVENING IN DANDALOO

It was while we held our races—
Hurdles, sprints and steeplechases—
  Up in Dandaloo,
That a crowd of Sydney stealers,
Jockeys, pugilists and spielers
Brought some horses, real heelers,
  Came and put us through.

Beat our nags and won our money,
Made the game by no means funny,
  Made us rather blue;
When the racing was concluded,
Of our hard-earned coin denuded
Dandaloonies sat and brooded
  There in Dandaloo.

.   .   .   .   .   .

Night came down on Johnson's shanty
Where the grog was no way scanty,
  And a tumult grew
Till some wild, excited person
Galloped down the township cursing,
"Sydney push have mobbed Macpherson,
  Roll up, Dandaloo!"

Great St Denis! what commotion!
Like the rush of stormy ocean
  Fiery horsemen flew.
Dust and smoke and din and rattle,
Down the street they spurred their cattle
To the war-cry of the battle,
  "Wade in, Dandaloo!"

So the boys might have their fight out,
Johnson blew the bar-room light out,
  Then, in haste, withdrew.
And in darkness and in doubting
Raged the conflict and the shouting,
"Give the Sydney push a clouting,
  Go it, Dandaloo!"

Jack Macpherson seized a bucket,
Every head he saw he struck it—
   Struck in earnest, too;
And a man from Lower Wattle,
Whom a shearer tried to throttle,
Hit out freely with a bottle
   There in Dandaloo.

Skin and hair were flying thickly,
When a light was fetched, and quickly
   Brought a fact to view—
On the scene of the diversion
Every single, solid person
Come along to help Macpherson—
   All were Dandaloo!

When the list of slain was tabled—
Some were drunk and some disabled—
   Still we found it true.
In the darkness and the smother
We'd been belting one another;
Jack Macpherson bashed his brother
   There in Dandaloo.

So we drank, and all departed—
How the "mobbing" yarn was started
   No one ever knew—
And the stockmen tell the story
Of that conflict fierce and gory,
How he fought for love and glory
   Up in Dandaloo.

It's a proverb now, or near it—
At the races you can hear it,
   At the dog-fights, too!
Every shrieking, dancing drover
As the canines topple over
Yells applause to Grip or Rover,
   "Give him 'Dandaloo'!"

And the teamster slowly toiling
Through the deep black country, soiling
   Wheels and axles, too,
Lays the whip on Spot and Banker,
Rouses Tarboy with a flanker—
"Redman! Ginger! Heave there! Yank her
   Wade in, Dandaloo!"

A BALLAD OF DUCKS

THE railway rattled and roared and swung
With jolting carriage and bumping trucks.
The sun, like a billiard red ball, hung
In the Western sky: and the tireless tongue
Of the wild-eyed man in the corner told
This terrible tale of the days of old,
And the party that ought to have kept the ducks.

"Well, it ain't all joy bein' on the land
With an overdraft that'd knock you flat;
And the rabbits have pretty well took command;
But the hardest thing for a man to stand
Is the feller who says 'Well, I told you so!
You should ha' done this way, don't you know!'—
I could lay a bait for a man like that.

"The grasshoppers struck us in ninety-one
And what they leave—well, it ain't *de luxe*.
But a growlin' fault-findin' son of a gun
Who'd lent some money to stock our run—
I said they'd eaten what grass we had—
Says he, 'Your management's very bad;
You had a right to have kept some ducks!'

"To have kept some ducks! And the place was white!
Wherever you went you had to tread
On grasshoppers guzzlin' day and night;
And then with a swoosh they rose in flight,
If you didn't look out for yourself they'd fly
Like bullets into your open eye
And knock it out of the back of your head.

"There isn't a turkey or goose or swan,
Or a duck that quacks, or a hen that clucks,
Can make a difference on a run
When a grasshopper plague has once begun;
'If you'd finance us,' I says, 'I'd buy
Ten thousand emus and have a try;
The job,' I says, 'is too big for ducks!

" 'You must fetch a duck when you come to stay;
A great big duck—a Muscovy toff—
Ready and fit,' I says, 'for the fray;
And if the grasshoppers come our way
You turn your duck into the lucerne patch,
And I'd be ready to make a match
That the grasshoppers eat his feathers off!'

"He came to visit us by and by,
And it just so happened one day in spring
A kind of a cloud came over the sky—
A wall of grasshoppers nine miles high,
And nine miles thick, and nine hundred wide,
Flyin' in regiments, side by side,
And eatin' up every living thing.

"All day long, like a shower of rain,
You'd hear 'em smackin' against the wall,
Tap, tap, tap, on the window pane,
And they'd rise and jump at the house again
Till their crippled carcasses piled outside.
But what did it matter if thousands died—
A million wouldn't be missed at all.

'We were drinkin' grasshoppers—so to speak—
Till we skimmed their carcasses off the spring;
And they fell so thick in the station creek
They choked the waterholes all the week.
There was scarcely room for a trout to rise,
And they'd only take artificial flies—
They got so sick of the real thing.

"An Arctic snowstorm was beat to rags
When the hoppers rose for their morning flight
With the flapping noise like a million flags:
And the kitchen chimney was stuffed with bags
For they'd fall right into the fire, and fry
Till the cook sat down and began to cry—
And never a duck or fowl in sight!

"We strolled across to the railroad track—
Under a cover beneath some trucks,
I sees a feather and hears a quack;
I stoops and I pulls the tarpaulin back—
Every duck in the place was there,
No good to them was the open air.
'Mister,' I says, 'There's your blanky ducks!'"

TOMMY
CORRIGAN

(Killed, Steeplechasing at Flemington.)

You talk of riders on the flat, of nerve and pluck and pace—
Not one in fifty has the nerve to ride a steeplechase.
It's right enough, while horses pull and take their fences strong,
To rush a flier to the front and bring the field along;
But what about the last half-mile, with horses blown and beat—
When every jump means all you know to keep him on his feet.

When any slip means sudden death—with wife and child to keep—
It needs some nerve to draw the whip and flog him at the leap—
But Corrigan would ride them out, by danger undismayed,
He never flinched at fence or wall, he never was afraid;
With easy seat and nerve of steel, light hand and smiling face,
He held the rushing horses back, and made the sluggards race.

He gave the shirkers extra heart, he steadied down the rash,
He rode great clumsy boring brutes, and chanced a fatal smash;
He got the rushing Wymlet home that never jumped at all—
But clambered over every fence and clouted every wall.
You should have heard the cheers, my boys, that shook the members'
     stand
Whenever Tommy Corrigan weighed out to ride Lone Hand.

They were, indeed, a glorious pair—the great upstanding horse,
The gamest jockey on his back that ever faced a course.
Though weight was big and pace was hot and fences stiff and tall,
"You follow Tommy Corrigan" was passed to one and all.
And every man on Ballarat raised all he could command
To put on Tommy Corrigan when riding old Lone Hand.

But now we'll keep his memory green while horsemen come and go;
We may not see his like again where silks and satins glow.
We'll drink to him in silence, boys—he's followed down the track
Where many a good man went before, but never one came back.
And, let us hope, in that far land where the shades of brave men
     reign,
The gallant Tommy Corrigan will ride Lone Hand again.

THE MAORI'S
WOOL

Now, this is just a simple tale to tell the reader how
They civilized the Maori tribe at Rooti-iti-au.

. . . . . .

THE Maoris are a mighty race—the finest ever known;
Before the missionaries came they worshipped wood and stone;
They went to war and fought like fiends, and when the war was
    done
They pacified their conquered foes by eating every one.
But now-a-days about the pahs in idleness they lurk,
Prepared to smoke or drink or talk—or anything but work.
The richest tribe in all the North in sheep and horse and cow,
Were those who led their simple lives at Rooti-iti-au.

'Twas down to town at Wellington a noble Maori came,
A Rangatira of the best, Rerenga was his name—
(The word Rerenga means a "snag"—but until he was gone
This didn't strike the folk he met—it struck them later on).
He stalked into the Bank they call the "Great Financial Hell",
And told the Chief Financial Fiend the tribe had wool to sell.
The Bold Bank Manager looked grave—the price of wool was high.
He said, "We'll lend you what you need—we're not disposed to buy.

"You ship the wool to England, Chief!—You'll find it's good advice,
And meanwhile you can draw from us the local market price."
The Chief he thanked him courteously and said he wished to state
In all the Rooti-iti tribe his mana would be great,
But still the tribe were simple folk, and did not understand
This strange finance that gave them cash without the wool in hand.
So off he started home again, with trouble on his brow,
To lay the case before the tribe at Rooti-iti-au.

They held a great korero in the Rooti-iti clan,
With speeches lasting half a day from every leading man.
They called themselves poetic names—"lost children in a wood";
They said the Great Bank Manager was Kapai—extra good!
And so they sent Rerenga down, full-powered and well-equipped,
To draw as much as he could get, and let the wool be shipped;
And wedged into a "Cargo Tank", full up from stern to bow,
A mighty clip of wool went Home from Rooti-iti-au.

It was the Bold Bank Manager who drew a heavy cheque;
Rerenga cashed it thoughtfully, then clasped him round the neck;
A hug from him was not at all a thing you'd call a lark—
You see he lived on mutton-birds and dried remains of shark—
But still it showed his gratitude; and, as he pouched the pelf,
"I'll haka for you, sir," he said, "in honour of yourself!"
The haka is a striking dance—the sort they don't allow
In any place more civilized than Rooti-iti-au.

He "haka'd" most effectively—then, with an airy grace,
Rubbed noses with the Manager, and vanished into space.
But when the wool return came back, ah me, what sighs and groans!
For every bale of Maori wool was loaded up with stones!
Yes—thumping great New Zealand rocks among the wool they
        found;
On every rock the Bank had lent just eighteen-pence a pound.
And now the Bold Bank Manager, with trouble on his brow,
Is searching vainly for the chief from Rooti-iti-au.

SUNRISE
ON THE COAST

Grey dawn on the sand-hills—the night wind has drifted
    All night from the rollers a scent of the sea;
With the dawn the grey fog his battalions has lifted,
    At the call of the morning they scatter and flee.

Like mariners calling the roll of their number
    The sea-fowl put out to the infinite deep.
And far overhead—sinking softly to slumber—
    Worn out by their watching the stars fall asleep.

To eastward, where rests the broad dome of the skies on
    The sea-line, stirs softly the curtain of night;
And far from behind the enshrouded horizon
    Comes the voice of a God saying "Let there be light."

And lo, there is light! Evanescent and tender,
    It glows ruby-red where 'twas now ashen-grey;
And purple and scarlet and gold in its splendour—
    Behold, 'tis that marvel, the birth of a day!

SONG OF
THE PEN

Not for the love of women toil we, we of the craft,
    Not for the people's praise;
Only because our goddess made us her own and laughed,
    Claiming us all our days,

Claiming our best endeavour—body and heart and brain
    Given with no reserve—
Niggard is she towards us, granting us little gain:
    Still, we are proud to serve.

Not unto us is given choice of the tasks we try,
    Gathering grain or chaff;
One of her favoured servants toils at an epic high,
    One, that a child may laugh.

Yet if we serve her truly in our appointed place,
    Freely she doth accord
Unto her faithful servants always this saving grace,
    Work is its own reward!

INDEX
TO FIRST LINES